... Brenna's confused thoughts focused on Sitting Bull's words, "When the Buffalo Calf Maiden return, she'll wear around her neck the lost *piedra de toque*."

Although her Christian faith refuted any thought that the touchstone could have any power, still she couldn't help thinking the *piedra de toque* was going to have a tremendous effect on her life.

Meadowsong Romances for your reading pleasure:

Freedom's Call   Irene B. Brand

Forbidden Legacy   Barbara A. Masci

Captured Heart   Barbara A. Masci

THE TOUCHSTONE

IRENE B. BRAND

Power Books

Fleming H. Revell
Old Tappan, New Jersey

Scripture quotations in this volume are from the King James Version of the Bible.

Library of Congress Cataloging-in-Publication Data

Brand, Irene B., date
  The touchstone / Irene B. Brand.
      p.   cm.
  ISBN 0-8007-5345-3
  I. Title.
PS3552.R2917T68   1990
813'.54—dc20   89-70031
                                          CIP

Copyright © 1990 by Irene B. Brand
Published by the Fleming H. Revell Company
Old Tappan, New Jersey 07675
Printed in the United States of America

TO
The 1988–89 staff
of
PPJHS

Prologue
1541

*S*and and tumbleweed breezed across the path of several giant, plodding beasts. Men, covered with armor and woolen capes, hunched over the animals' backs, shielding their faces from the driving rain and hail that bounced off the steel helmets.

Eyes wide with wonder, a native monitored the riders. Never before had he seen such creatures—big dogs carrying men on their backs! His furry garment blended into the sand as he stealthily followed the strangers, and the riders remained unaware of their observer.

A herd of buffalo drifted into view, and the strange men urged their animals forward, shouting words the native didn't understand. Black smoke erupted from the cylindrical objects the men carried, and the simultaneous thunder startled the native. The noise also spooked the buffalo, who began to lumber across the prairie. One rider fell beneath the hooves of the stampeding animals.

Brown hands pulled the man behind a bush. As death hovered over the fallen stranger he groaned piteously. Fumbling hands drew forth a gold chain from his garments, and

as his life ebbed, he caressed the black, polished stone attached to the chain.

"Piedra de toque, piedra de toque," he whispered over and
over.

Hearing the strange humans returning, the native jerked
the *piedra de toque* from the man's grasp and fled. The explor-
ers lifted their fallen comrade into his saddle and turned
southward.

The wind continued its relentless onslaught, spreading
rain and hail across the barren land, but huddling in his
grass hut, the native paid no heed to the elements. *"Piedra de
toque,"* he stammered slowly as he clasped the jewel in his
hands. Possession of the stone brought him a sensation of
peace and power.

1

*S*crewdriver and pliers in hand, Brenna Anderson purposefully climbed the stairs to her parents' bedroom, followed by her maid, Mendy. Halting at the threshold, Brenna closed her eyes to hold back the smarting tears.

"Can't hardly believe they're dead," Mendy voiced Brenna's thoughts. "Just a week ago, they started off so happy to attend that convention, and wham, a train wreck, and now they're dead and buried. Philadelphia just won't be the same without 'em."

Brenna paused beside the chest of drawers that matched the massive ornately carved bed, and with trembling hands, she lifted a double gilt frame.

Her own face stared back at her. The artist had caught the expression her parents had loved—sparkling, dancing eyes, a hint of a smile ready to break on her angular, russet face. Black hair, lifted high on her head, was slightly darker than the deep-set eyes. She sensed determination in her face, maybe because her father, John Anderson, had assured Brenna that her firm cleft chin indicated strength of character.

I hope he was right. I need all the strength I can muster now. She glanced at the other photograph in the frame, the one of her parents taken on the same day, two years ago on Brenna's eighteenth birthday.

Easy to tell that she wasn't an Anderson by birth—she had none of their physical characteristics. But as Brenna knelt beside the squat, leather-bound trunk at the foot of the bed, she hoped she'd developed their resourcefulness and integrity.

With fingers that seemed stiff and helpless, she inserted the screwdriver under the trunk's lid.

"You're goin' to ruin that trunk," Mendy warned nervously.

"Do you know any other way to open it?"

The black woman shook her head. "No, but I'd think you'd want to have it for a keepsake. Yore pa brought that back with him from the West, same time he brought you."

"I know. That's the reason I'm determined to break it open. Or," and she turned suspiciously to Mendy, "do you know where there's a key for it?"

"Mebbe. There's a ring of old keys around here someplace."

"If you don't know where they are, I'll not wait for you to find them. If I break the lock, I'll have it repaired." Nervously she pried upward on the lid.

"Ever hear of Pandora, Mendy?"

"Don't think so."

"She opened a box once and let all kinds of evil loose in the world. That may be what I'll do, but I hope this trunk holds some hint about my past. With Mom and Dad gone, I'm afraid I'll never know anything about my *real* identity."

Mendy nodded sagely. "You've always been a mystery child. Mister John brought you when he come home from that Indian agency out in Nebraska, back in seventy. Since

Miz Susan had just lost her own little one, she was tickled to git you.''

Mendy helped Brenna force the lid open, but at first the contents yielded nothing unusual. They glanced at papers John had collected from his students when he'd taught at the Red Cloud Agency. Carefully they unwrapped Susan's wedding dress, which she'd kept for Brenna to wear someday. Brenna laid aside a copy of the Psalms without opening it.

Finally, from the bottom of the trunk, she lifted a buckskin bag, tied with leather thongs. Seven circles, divided into pie-shaped sections painted white, red, black, and yellow, decorated the bag's surface. Sight of those uneven designs caused Brenna's heart to flutter, and she closed her eyes.

"Ain't that like the mark on yore arm?" Mendy quizzed. Drawing up the sleeve of Brenna's dress, she exposed a small tattooed circle near the girl's right armpit.

Brenna seldom thought about the strange mark on her arm, though it had been there as long as she could remember. As she'd grown older, the circle had faded somewhat, but it was still vivid enough to reveal its similarity to the markings on the bag.

Mendy took the pouch, untied the leather strings, and spread it before Brenna.

"Looks like baby shoes," Mendy commented as Brenna lifted a small pair of fur-lined moccasins embroidered with crude animal figures. When Brenna picked up a rolled skin, a long golden chain fell out.

"Ain't that purty?" Mendy said.

Brenna stared at the polished black stone dangling from the chain. The jewel covered the palm of her hand, and the light from the window reflected on a few faint gold streaks across the ebony surface.

On a piece of skin attached to the necklace, Brenna deciphered some crooked, scrawling letters, "For my dotter."

"I don't understand," she said. "This must be an expensive necklace. Why would Dad leave it lying in this trunk for years?"

The maid shook her head. "I don't know. 'Course Mr. John didn't tell all he knew—not even to Miz Susan."

Brenna laid all the other items back in the trunk and closed the lid, but she carried the leather bag and its contents into her room. Pulling a rocking chair close to the fireplace, she sat with the bag on her lap.

The last time she'd questioned her parents about her ancestry, John Anderson had said, "You're our child, and for now, that's all you need to know. When you're twenty-one, we'll tell you everything. Until then, let us go on loving you as our own."

She hadn't mentioned the matter to them again, but now she yearned to find out who she *really* was. Unbidden, some link with the past tugged at her heart, forcing her toward a step that she feared yet knew she must take. *Did Indian blood flow in her veins?*

"Just call me Pandora," she muttered.

Mendy knocked lightly on the door, and said, "Lawyer Casto will be here soon, missy. You'd better come downstairs."

Picking up the Indian items, Brenna wandered down to her father's office. While she waited for the lawyer, Brenna opened the rolltop desk to gather the papers Mr. Casto had asked her to have ready.

She lifted a bulging brown envelope marked *History of the Sioux Nation*. It contained a book outline, but only one chapter of the book had been written.

"Poor Dad," she murmured. "He waited too long to write his book." Frequently, John had talked about publishing a book on the Plains Indians, but his duties at the nearby Quaker college had left him little time for writing. The book would never be written now.

When a knock sounded on the front door, Mendy waddled down the hall to admit Allen Casto, a longtime friend of John Anderson. Short, fat, and unprepossessing, the man's appearance did little to warrant his reputation as an excellent attorney.

Casto greeted Brenna warmly, handed his coat to Mendy, and opened his briefcase. "Even though the deaths of John and Susan were untimely, he had business affairs in order, and there will be nothing for you to worry about," he comforted her.

The attorney drew several papers from his case and handed one to Brenna. "Here's a copy of the will for you to read at your leisure, but I'll briefly explain the terms."

Brenna quickly scanned the document's pages, dated July, 1889, less than a year ago, but the words told her nothing she didn't already know.

"As you can see, all of the estate will become yours, except a legacy to Mendy and a larger contribution to the Carlisle Indian School."

Those two bequests didn't surprise Brenna, for Mendy had worked at the Andersons' for years, and she'd been a close friend as well as a maid. And John Anderson had been interested in the welfare of native Americans since he'd worked for the Bureau of Indian Affairs in his youth.

"However, there is an account at the bank that is yours already." Brenna stared at the lawyer in shock.

Casto riffled some sheets, avoiding her eyes. "Your father had one account that totals over $50,000, in your name alone, with John and myself as joint trustees until you became of age."

"But where did this money come from? Why didn't Dad use it? I know many times he had to count every penny to find the money to pay the expenses for my education."

"The account was opened in 1870, and the interest has accumulated. John didn't use the account, apparently."

"And you don't know where he obtained the money?"

"No, I don't. The day he wrote his will, he transferred the money to you, asking me to serve as joint trustee, so that I could administer the account in the event of his death. You'll be twenty-one in three months, and by that time, we should be able to settle the whole estate. In the meantime, if you need money for living expenses, either the bank or I will advance you necessary funds. Now, is there anything else I can do for you, Brenna?"

Stifling the qualm that urged caution, Brenna made a quick decision and handed the buckskin bag to Casto. "These items were in an old trunk in Dad's room. Can you tell me anything about them?"

She monitored Casto's countenance apprehensively as he examined the bag, the moccasins, and the necklace. He held the piece of skin with the message on it for minutes before he looked into Brenna's worried eyes.

"No, I've never seen these. I know nothing about them." He paused again—for hours, it seemed to Brenna. "You do know that you're an adopted child."

"Yes, they never made any secret about that, but when I asked questions about my real parents, Dad said to wait until I was twenty-one."

Casto looked at her compassionately. "But are you sure you want to know? The Andersons gave you so much, and you've been happy as their daughter. Why pry into the past? Are you *sure* you want to know?"

Brenna glanced around the room and thought, *It's a goodly heritage*, but this was no time for indecision.

"I want to know." She wondered if it were her voice that spoke or the chant of some long-gone ancestor, but as she heard the words, she realized she'd started on a course of no return.

The next morning, Brenna hired a hack and headed for the business center of Philadelphia, directing the driver to a jewelry store on Market Street. As she entered the store, her hands touched the black necklace, which felt heavy as a rock, hanging inside her bodice.

She'd known this jeweler for a long time, and her parents had considered him trustworthy. "I found this article in my parents' belongings," she explained, removing the necklace and handing it to him, "and I need to have it appraised. Are you able to help me?"

The jeweler lifted the stone close to his eyeglass, and scrutinized it critically. "It's obviously black jade, but these gold streaks are unusual." He lowered the necklace and gave it back to Brenna. "Somewhere recently I've seen something like this. Watch the shop while I run upstairs to my living quarters."

A wall clock ticked off the minutes, and Brenna thumped her hand on the glass-topped counter, in rhythm to the swinging pendulum. She barely noticed the display of diamond rings that blinked at her.

Excitement tinged the jeweler's face as he rustled into the room. "I thought I'd read something about such a stone. Look at this."

He held a jewelry catalog turned to a page of antique pieces. Even Brenna's untrained eye saw the resemblance between her necklace and the one illustrated in the book.

"You have a *piedra de toque*—that's Spanish for a touchstone."

"A touchstone? Doesn't that have something to do with gold?"

"A touchstone is a black siliceous stone, usually some kind of quartz, used to ascertain the purity of gold and silver. After it's used awhile, the touchstone takes on gold and silver streaks. Black jade with gold stripes resembles a touchstone, hence the name. According to this catalog, jewelry made from this type of jade was carried from the East by the Crusaders. Only a few of these jewels are still around today—most of them are in museums. You have a priceless antique here."

The jeweler laughed as he placed the catalog under the counter. "Maybe I shouldn't tell you this, but I understand that certain mystical powers are associated with that necklace."

"What kind of mystical powers?"

"Its possessor will be assured of wealth and power."

He laughed again, and Brenna with him, but her mirth was hollow. A chill started at her neck and slithered down her spine when she thought of the big bank account she now owned.

Brenna spent a restless night, wondering, *Is the touchstone a bad omen?* More than once she considered throwing the jewel out the window. As daylight filtered into the room, Brenna stared upward at the half-tester-top bed, and said to herself, *I'll go crazy if I don't unravel this mystery.*

Where could she start? If John Anderson had brought her with him when he returned from the Indian agency in Nebraska, that seemed the logical place to learn what she wanted to know. Still, she needed some excuse to go west. Suddenly she conceived an idea: *Why couldn't I finish the book on the Sioux that my father had started?* Why not, indeed! She could go west with the outward purpose of writing about the Sioux, while her hidden motive would be to search out her ancestry.

2

"*I*f you go way out there, I'm goin', too."

Brenna suppressed a smile, for she'd expected this reaction when Mendy learned that she planned to go west in a few weeks.

"You'll do nothing of the kind. Lot I'd accomplish on writing a book if I had to look after you."

"Now, Miss Brenna, it just ain't fitting for a young lady to travel by herself. Miz Susan would expect me to look after you."

"I don't happen to need a chaperone, Miss Mendy."

"I'm a-goin'."

"Indians will scalp you. You sure would look funny without that mop of hair."

Mendy's eyes bulged, but she stood firm. "You can't scare me away. You go, I go."

"And after they scalp you," Brenna continued, as if she hadn't spoken, "they'll put you in a big pot, boil you until you're tender, then eat you."

Mendy started violently. "You stop that kind of talk, 'fore you make me mad. I'm goin'."

All along Brenna had intended to take Mendy with her, but if she hadn't approached it this way, Mendy would have refused.

"Well, if you're determined to go where you aren't wanted, you'd better start making plans. I intend to leave the end of March."

"We goin' where that little Injun girl lives? I'd like to see her again."

"We'll be in that area, and I've written her a note to tell her our plans. If I can contact her, she might be a lot of help to me. She won't be such a little girl now; she was fifteen when she visited us, and that was over three years ago."

In 1886, White Dove, a Sioux student at the Carlisle Indian School, had lived in the Andersons' home for two months, as a part of the school's goal to "kill the Indian and save the man." Brenna and Dove had become good friends. They'd exchanged a few letters at first, but Brenna hadn't heard from Dove for over two years.

Then Brenna's mind wandered to the day she met Kirby Chapman, Dove's stepbrother, who came to accompany the Indian girl back to Nebraska. One day Brenna had answered a knock at the door, gazed up into his face, and she hadn't been the same since.

Kirby's crisp russet hair waved back from his forehead, steel-blue eyes gleamed from his deeply tanned face, and his frank, friendly smile radiated a charm that captivated Brenna. Kirby towered a few inches over John Anderson, who was six feet tall, and his thigh and shoulder muscles rippled with well-controlled power, but in spite of his size, the young man walked with a light, jaunty step.

During most of his overnight visit, Anderson had monopolized Kirby, but Brenna and Dove had taken him to a circus performing in a park near their home. They'd snacked on peanuts and lemonade and had enjoyed a beautiful afternoon. Since Kirby was eight years her senior, Brenna supposed he'd never given her another thought, but he'd remained the "man of her dreams." Her pulse quickened at the thought of seeing him again.

After sifting through her father's notes on the Sioux, Brenna decided to take only the outline he'd made. She pondered long over a statement John had jotted down on one sheet. "Note the similarities between Sioux religion and Christianity. Is it possible to take the deep-seated fervor of these people and lead them to Christ?"

Brenna's father had conducted Christian worship for the Indians at the agency, and had agonized over their lack of response. As she packed the manuscript she determined to learn all she could about the Sioux religion. Perhaps she could also continue that work her father had started.

A letter from White Dove would have given Brenna a more secure feeling, but no message arrived before she and Mendy set out on the first of April. Although she didn't want Mendy to know, Brenna had suffered many misgivings about the trip. What if she couldn't communicate with the Indians about their culture? What if she learned unpleasant facts about her past?

After a week of travel, Brenna and Mendy boarded a train for the last lap of their journey to Crawford, Nebraska. With a sigh, Brenna settled down on the ragged cushions of the passengers' car. The train quivered and jerked along the tracks, and Brenna, already tired, didn't anticipate the next two days with any joy.

Knowing she had to endure the discomfort until they arrived in Crawford, she looked out the windows in an attempt to still her impatience. Gone were the rolling hills of Iowa. Nebraska seemed like a different world—an arid land of sparse habitation. When they stopped at small towns, Brenna looked with interest at the people who boarded. She eyed the few Indians especially, some dressed in white man's garments, others wearing buffalo robes over their shoulders. Brenna's pulse quickened when she noted that the designs painted on their garments matched those on her deerskin bag.

When an Indian woman, carrying a child, sat across the aisle from her, Brenna tried to engage the woman in conversation.

"What's the baby's name?" she asked.

The woman turned startled eyes upon Brenna and moved closer to the window.

"You have a nice baby," Brenna tried again.

"*Hoye,*" the woman muttered.

"Do you understand English?"

"*Hoye.*"

"What does *hoye* mean?" Brenna mumbled. In exasperation, she fished in her briefcase for a list of Sioux words her dad had compiled.

"*Hoye* means 'yes,' " Brenna said to Mendy, who'd been monitoring the attempted conversation with disapproval.

Though Brenna tried several other comments, each time she received *hoye* for an answer, and finally the woman moved to another car.

Brenna had more luck with a burly rancher and his wife, who boarded the train at Valentine, en route to Chadron. The rancher spoke to her, while his wife turned curious eyes upon them. Waving her hand toward the bumpy hills covered with brown waving grass and clumps of evergreens, Brenna said, "Tell me something about this enchanting country."

"It ain't never enchanted me," the woman responded grimly. "For ten years we've tried to eke out a living on our spread, and it's been nip and tuck all the time."

"Now, Emmie, it ain't all bad. These are sand hills out here, ma'am," the rancher said as he turned to Brenna. "At first we tried to farm our section of land, but that was a mistake. Not enough moisture to farm the way we did back in Missouri, and the wind blew the dried earth away."

"Life ain't no easier now that we're grazin' cattle."

"That's right, but we're making some money at it. 'Course my ranch is pretty small potatoes, but some mighty big spreads have sprung up in Dawes County. Mighty big spreads!

"Where are you headed, miss?" the rancher asked.

"Crawford."

The woman turned startled eyes toward Brenna, then shifted her gaze to Mendy. Hurriedly, she picked up her satchel and prepared to move, but her husband pushed his wife back on the seat.

"Set down, Emmie. You're always putting the worst light on everything. You can tell by looking at them that they ain't loose women."

Mendy moaned, and Brenna laughed aloud.

"It ain't funny, Miss Brenna," Mendy hissed.

"No offense meant, miss," the rancher apologized. "But seein' that the majority of buildings in Crawford are saloons and bawdy houses, Emmie just made a natural mistake. Ain't many decent women in Crawford."

"Miss Brenna, what kind of place have you brought us to? Miz Susan would turn over in her grave if she knew where we are now."

"Well, she doesn't know, and I'm not worried about it."

When the town of Chadron was called, the rancher and his wife trudged down the aisle with a wave of their hands. Mendy and Brenna silently watched the boarding passengers, and Mendy stared at two uniformed Negroes who passed down the aisle.

"Wonder what those soldiers are doin' out here?" she whispered.

"Fort Robinson, at Crawford, is the headquarters for the

Ninth Cavalry; that's a regiment of Negro soldiers. Chances are, you'll find a beau."

"I ain't interested in no man, but I want you to know, if I took it into my head, I ain't too old for a beau. I'm not forty-five yet."

"Not yet, but almost, if I remember right."

Mendy merely tossed her head.

Brenna's first sight of Crawford wasn't reassuring. She'd been steeling herself for squalor, after seeing the towns en route, but the dilapidated sidewalks, the dusty streets, and the ill-kempt, staring men made her want to turn and run for home. There wasn't a woman in sight!

After his first shock at seeing them, the station agent offered his help. When she stated her intention of going to a hotel, he gasped, "My word, miss, this ain't no time for you to be in a hotel. It's payday for the Ninth Cavalry, and this town will be roaring tonight. Ain't there anybody you know in Crawford where you could go?"

"I don't know anyone here. Surely there's a decent hotel?"

"Oh, the hotel is decent enough, and some of us can take you there safe and sound, but stay inside behind locked doors tonight."

The agent called one of the loafers sitting on the depot's porch. "Say, Ezra, how about taking these *ladies* and their trunks to the hotel."

After sitting for days without exercise, Brenna welcomed the walk to the hotel, but when a gunshot sounded in the direction they headed, she longed for the security of Philadelphia. Mendy clung to Brenna's arm, fearfully looking over her shoulder.

Two drunken black soldiers planted themselves in Mendy's path, and one of them said, "Daisy, are we glad to see you! Where you gonna set up business?" He reached out and grabbed Mendy's arm, and she screamed. Brenna swung the briefcase she carried and struck the man on the head.

"Leave her alone," she ordered, and when Ezra, who was behind them with the luggage, shouted, "Stop it! They're ladies," the two soldiers staggered away.

Brenna sighed with relief when they entered the brick-front hotel. The proprietor didn't bother to conceal his curiosity, but he didn't question them about their presence in Crawford. He showed Brenna a room over the dining area—a barren room smelling of cooked cabbage, which was fairly clean, and Brenna agreed to take it.

"Please put a cot in here for my maid, and send up our supper in an hour. We'll also need water for bathing."

After they'd eaten the meal of steak and potatoes that an Indian woman brought them, Brenna turned the key in the flimsy door and decided it was scant protection, so they moved the dresser in front of the door before they went to bed.

Sounds of revelry from the street kept Brenna awake most of the night, but no one came near them, and by morning she decided she had nothing to fear in Crawford. After they'd eaten, Brenna left Mendy to launder their traveling clothes, and she headed out into town, hoping to find someone to advise her about visiting the Indian reservation.

While she poised indecisively on the sidewalk, a vehicle drawn by two swift-stepping sorrels wheeled down the street. She looked in appreciation at the team, not seeing the occupants of the vehicle.

When she heard someone call her name, Brenna noticed a dark-skinned girl sitting on the seat of the conveyance. The girl's shining black hair, divided in a straight line to the nape of her neck, hung below her shoulders. *White Dove!*

The Indian girl jumped into the street and rushed to Brenna. "Good to see you again."

"And I'm glad to see you. How'd you know I was here?"

"Your letter didn't come in time to answer, but one of the

ranch hands was in town when you arrived last night. He brought the news to the Bar C. We've come to fetch you."

"We?" Brenna said, looking quickly at Dove's companion, who had tied the horses to an iron rail.

"Yes. This is Stuart King, the Bar-C foreman. He volunteered to come in for you. Never misses a chance to meet a pretty girl."

Standing ramrod straight and towering over Dove, Stuart King was past his youth, probably in his fifties, Brenna decided. He seemed pleasant, and Brenna liked the lift of his chin and the steadiness of his gray eyes.

He removed his hat and reached for her hand. "I've heard about you, miss, from Dove. You two must've been pretty good friends when she was back East."

"Now it's our turn to entertain you at the Bar C," Dove said. "Where are your trunks?"

"Oh, I wouldn't think of imposing on you. I have a room at the hotel." Brenna panicked momentarily. The Bar C meant Kirby Chapman, and she didn't think it was wise to pay an extended visit to his house. She didn't want to do anything foolish.

"You remember Kirby, don't you? He sent us for you. You're to be his guest at the ranch."

"Besides, Crawford is no place for a woman alone," Stuart added.

"But I'm not alone—Mendy came with me. You remember Mendy, Dove?"

Dove's eyes brightened. "I remember good food she made. But Mendy may come to the ranch, too. She can help my mother with the cooking."

In a matter of an hour, with their trunks loaded into the buckboard, Crawford was left behind.

"Did you have any trouble in Crawford last night? We didn't like the idea of your being in there alone. Crawford's not too bad, except on payday at the fort, and then anything might happen," Stuart stated.

"No trouble at all. The station agent warned us it would be a wild night, so we stayed hidden and kept our doors locked. But I didn't sleep much."

Dove leaned forward. "Brown came into town as soon as we learned you arrived. He found out where you were and kept guard all night. So you were safer than you thought."

"Brown?"

"My brother. He went to Carlisle, too, but he lives at the ranch now."

"The ranch lies thirty miles east of Crawford," Stuart explained. "We'll be there in less than two hours, so enjoy your trip."

After the shabbiness of Crawford and the primitive sod houses she'd seen along the railroad route, Brenna was amazed at the stately Bar-C ranch house that dominated the landscape. The multigabled Queen Anne house gleamed bright yellow in the sunlight. A columned front veranda broadened into a tiled rotunda on the side, and in contrast, the other log buildings, while serviceable, lacked the splendor of the ranch house. Many cattle roamed the pastures, searching for food in the lush creek bottoms.

When Stuart pulled up in front of the house, two men rose from the wicker furniture on the rotunda and came down the steps. Brenna had eyes only for Kirby, whose appearance proved that her dreams had all been true.

"Welcome to the Bar-C ranch, Miss Anderson. I've looked forward to meeting you again." The warmth of his greeting unnerved Brenna, and she wondered, *Has he also thought about me for three years?* She had trouble holding his warm gaze, and Brenna switched her attention to Kirby's companion.

Standing almost as tall as Kirby, the man beside him had

the features of an Indian. Dressed in a woolen shirt and trousers, his shoulder-length black hair fell from a beaded headband. An arched nose dominated his broad face, and his full mouth spread into a slight smile as he extended his hand.

"This is Brown Bear, Dove's brother," Kirby introduced him. If she had any Indian blood, as Brenna suspected, it stirred at that moment. How else could she explain the stimulus that bolted up her arm when Brown touched her?

Without understanding why, she knew that of the two men she'd just greeted, the meeting with Brown Bear made the greater impression upon her. She gazed into his eyes, until she felt her face reddening, and she welcomed Kirby's voice, "Come inside. Dove will show you to your room."

"We need to find a place for Brenna's maid, Mendy," Dove said. "Is all right for her to stay here?"

"Certainly," Kirby agreed. "Talk to your mother. There's plenty of room."

He took Brenna's arm and drew her inside. Kirby's touch tantalized her composure, but Brenna was acutely aware of Brown's magnetic personality, and she turned to watch him as he walked down the steps toward the buckboard. He glanced backwards, and their gazes caught and held for a tense moment, until he lifted his hand in silent farewell.

3

*D*ove showed Brenna to the round room over the front porch.

"Nice room," Dove said, pulling back the lace curtains from the curved double windows.

The view included the ranch buildings and the rolling hills beyond. Brenna spotted Brown at once, straddling a black horse and racing away from the corral. Shunning the temptation to watch him, Brenna turned hurriedly to look at the room.

The walls glowed in their covering of light-pink wallpaper, embossed with random sprays of white roses. The brass bedstead looked plump and cozy, with its puffy feather mattress covered with a white lace spread. An oak washstand held a bowl and pitcher, and on the shelf underneath, Brenna spotted a chamber pot.

"Where's your room?"

"Right across the hall. Kirby's room is beyond mine. Brown sleeps in the bunkhouse with the ranch hands.

"This has been my home since I came home from Carlisle," Dove continued. "My mother married Mr. Chapman

27

the first year I went away. I have a little room at the school-house in Pine Ridge, and I stay there most of the time, when school's in session."

"You're happy here?"

"Yes. I thought when Mr. Chapman died that my mother would move back to the reservation, but she seems content to stay, and Brown and I get along all right with Kirby. Brown is not always happy here; he thinks he betrays his ancestors to live as a white man, but so far, he has stayed."

"Brown is older than you?"

Dove dropped down on the oval woolen rug beside the bed, watching while Mendy brushed and arranged Brenna's hair.

"By seven years. He went to Carlisle a few years ahead of me, but we came home the same season. He worked for the army at Camp Robinson as a guide, but he's the best worker with horses on the ranch, so Kirby values his help."

Brenna hadn't expected the Indians to sit at the table with her and Kirby, but when she and Dove went to the dining room, Kirby and Brown rose to meet them. Where was the friction she'd understood existed between whites and Indi-ans?

After Kirby prayed God's blessing on the food, a tall In-dian woman entered the room, and Dove said, "Brenna, this is my mother, Tatoke."

The woman, dressed in a multicolored sateen dress, gave Brenna a brief smile and nodded as she set plates of food on the table. Mendy bustled in behind her, carrying a pot of coffee and a pitcher of milk. Apparently she'd fit right into the household, but Tatoke's position bothered Brenna; appar-ently Kirby's tolerance didn't extend to his stepmother.

Perhaps Dove sensed Brenna's discomfort, for she ex-plained, "Mother does not speak English much, and she's happier to wait on us. She does the cooking."

As she placed ample portions of the venison steak and

beans on her plate, Brenna wondered if Tatoke had been nothing more than a housekeeper when Kirby's father had lived, but the ease with which Brown and Dove fit into the family scene indicated that Kirby didn't bear any animosity toward his father's second wife.

"I guess we shouldn't question our good fortune in having you visit us, but may I ask why you're traveling in this area, Miss Anderson?" Kirby asked.

Even though the words sounded stilted, she said, "Please call me Brenna," and added, "as I told Dove in the letter, my parents were killed in a train accident two months ago, and I've come west to complete a project that my father has been planning for years. He had voluminous notes on the Sioux nation, and he'd planned to write a book about them. Since he died without realizing that dream, I'm going to write the book in his memory."

"*Wakantanka*, help us!" Brown exploded. "We have the archaeologist, the missionary, and the artist. All the Sioux need to finish us is a historian."

"Brown!" Dove pleaded.

Kirby gave him a warning look. "I doubt Brenna will write anything to harm the Sioux. Her father was always sympathetic to their needs."

"That's true," Brenna agreed hurriedly, trying not to note Brown's angry countenance. Why should she mind that he didn't approve of her work? "And even though he'd done lots of research, still I don't think I could take Dad's notes and write a book without looking over the field myself."

"That's good reasoning," Kirby agreed. "What are your plans?"

"I don't have any definite ones, except that I want to find a guide and interpreter to take me to the reservation this summer. I intend to make inquiries in Crawford."

"That shouldn't be too difficult," Kirby assured her. He grinned and glanced at Brown.

Not too busy with his steak to ignore the look, Brown threw up his hands. "Don't look at me, Kirby. You know the reservation. *You* take her."

"I'm running a ranch, remember?" Kirby countered.

"Oh, you two men! I'll take her myself," Dove said, turning to Brenna. "In a few weeks, my school'll be finished. Then we go."

"That's nice of you, Dove, but really I don't want to impose on you. I'd expected to hire a guide."

"Let's wait and see," Kirby said. "But you're going to see Sioux sooner than that. I had a message from Sitting Bull this morning that he intends to pass this way in a few days, and asked permission to visit the Bar C."

"Sitting Bull?" Brenna exclaimed. "Isn't he the one responsible for Custer's defeat?"

"Maybe. Maybe not," Brown responded. "Sitting Bull wasn't on the battlefield, but he made the 'big medicine' that helped Crazy Horse wipe out the Seventh Cavalry."

"I saw Sitting Bull a few years ago when he toured the East. When the tour came through Philadelphia, Dad took us to see him, but Dad became very angry when the leader of the group misinterpreted everything Sitting Bull said. He tried to tell the crowd that the interpretation was false, but they shouted him down. People believe what they want to, I guess."

Brown appraised her with a keen, perhaps more kindly glance. When she watched the way Brown handled his silver and noted his table manners, Brenna found it difficult to realize that the man opposite her was a full-blooded Indian. Though his native background showed in his speech, he wore his blue flannel shirt and Levis with ease. Remembering the satisfied gleam in his black eyes when he spoke of the tremendous Sioux victory at the Little Bighorn, he seemed every whit an Indian.

After they'd finished their dessert of peach cobbler and

whipped cream, Brenna preceded the rest into the living room, which held furnishings that matched the elegance of her own home. Paneled walls of varnished pine boards reached to the log-beamed ceiling. On the north wall, a huge stone fireplace reached almost to the ceiling, and fire crackled in its mammoth interior. Several fur rugs lay near the fireplace, and brown-toned Oriental rugs covered much of the other floor space. About a dozen reed chairs were grouped around the room.

"I guess I've received my comeuppance," Brenna commented to Kirby. "I thought I'd be coming to the frontier, but you've a beautiful home here."

"My mother can be thanked for that. When she first married Dad, they lived in a sod house, but she vowed that someday she'd have a fine home. Dad met Mother on a trip to Chicago once, fell in love with her, and persuaded her to come out here. I don't think she was ever happy, and to make it up to her, Dad built this house seven years ago and furnished it with everything she wanted. Though she only lived to enjoy it one year, it was worth the cost to Dad. And Tatoke has taken good care of everything, the way my mother did, so it is a nice home. We enjoy it."

She gave Kirby credit that he didn't seem to resent his father's remarriage. Yes, Kirby in the flesh was just as fine as her dreams had made him. *But*, she thought, with a glance at Brown, who stood looking out the window, *I wish he hadn't complicated everything.*

About eight o'clock, Stuart King wandered in for a visit. Settling into a reed chair by the fireplace, he said, "Been entertaining our guest with hair-raising stories, Kirby?"

"Nope. I'll leave that to you. Dad and you are the ones who had the wild experiences."

"How's that?" Brenna asked when Stuart chuckled.

"Bill Chapman and I met up with each other down in Texas, right after the Civil War. We worked down there for a while, and then we brought up a trail herd—one of the last ones on the Western Trail. When we got the critters to Ogallala, we didn't like the price the railroad demanded for freight, so we herded the cattle on north and took up a ranch here."

"How long ago was that?"

"Back in sixty-six. Bill settled down and became a prosperous rancher, but I hadn't done all the wandering I wanted to. One day, old and broke, I came back to the Bar C, riding the grub line, and Bill took me in."

"Yeah, that's a likely story," Kirby jeered. "How about that gold pocket you found while you lived with the Sioux? I'll bet you've still got that stashed away someplace."

"No, my boy, you're wrong—that gold has been gone a long time. I invested it in a good market, and I'm beginning to draw interest on it now."

"Brenna came west to gather information about the Sioux for a book. Think she can find what she wants?" Kirby asked.

"Why not? Sitting Bull is a story in himself. That's why I came up. Brown told me the old man is going to pay us a visit, and he won't come alone. What do you want me to do with them?"

"That pasture west of the corrals is empty now, so they can set up their tepees there. You'd better bring in several steers. They've probably had a lean winter. We'll invite Sitting Bull to eat up here with us—that will give Brenna a good chance to meet him."

Stuart unwound his long frame from the chair, smiled at Brenna and Dove, and took his departure.

"If you'll excuse me now, Brenna," Kirby said, "I need to discuss tomorrow's work with Stuart."

She watched his tall, straight back as he left the room and with difficulty brought her mind back to Dove.

"I'd like to go to my room now. I'm still not rested from that train trip, for with all the revelry in Crawford last night, I couldn't sleep much."

Dove nodded. "You plan to take it easy for next few days. We have plenty of time for visiting later. I'll go to Pine Ridge early in the morning, but school is only a half day, so I'll be back day after tomorrow."

After she undressed Brenna searched for her Bible. In spite of the warm welcome at the Bar C, she felt lonely tonight and missed her parents more than she had since the first few days after their deaths.

Brenna leafed aimlessly through the Bible's pages at first, seeking something to comfort her. Remembering Jacob and the first days of his exile from home, she turned to the book of Genesis. "And, behold, I am with thee, and will keep thee in all places whither thou goest, and will bring thee again into this land; for I will not leave thee, until I have done that which I have spoken to thee of. And Jacob awaked out of his sleep, and he said, Surely the Lord is in this place; and I knew it not."

Afterwards, she lay in the darkness and thought about the words. Surely God approved of her plan to bring the plight of the Sioux to the American people. In the face of His approval, she had the same promise of security He'd given Jacob. "I am with thee, and will keep thee in all places whither thou goest."

Jolted suddenly from sleep, Brenna sat up, alarmed.

"Wake up, Miss Brenna," Mendy shouted. "We're hemmed in by Injuns."

Brenna angrily shoved Mendy away. "Stop it! You know I don't like to be awakened like that." She gasped for breath, and her heartbeat raced.

"But I'm scared. Lookee." Mendy pulled her toward the window.

In a large field west of the house an Indian village had sprouted overnight. Brenna counted ten tepees, with thirty or more Indians milling around them. Blanketed horses and a few wagons stood around the tepees, and several Bar-C cowboys sat on the corral fence, watching the Indians.

"There's no cause for such a fuss," Brenna stated. "Kirby said last night that Sitting Bull would be here today."

"Who's that?"

Brenna left the window, and started stripping for the bath Mendy had already prepared. The room was cold, and she shivered as the warm water rose over her lower body.

"Sitting Bull is an important Sioux chief. Maybe he'll invite me to visit him on the reservation."

"You ain't got no business running around like that," Mendy mumbled. But busily soaping her body, Brenna ignored her.

"Tatoke say you'd best eat yore breakfast up here, 'cause everybody else is up and gone. I'll fetch it up soon."

"Are you getting along with Tatoke?"

"Uh-huh. She's a nice woman, but she don't talk much."

After Brenna dressed, Mendy started for the door with the bath water. "I'll bring up yore breakfast."

A note from Dove lay on the tray. "Make yourself at home," Brenna read. "Maybe one day, you'll go to school with me. That would be a good chance to watch Sioux while they study."

After breakfast, Brenna added a cloak over her poplin dress and even at that, when she stepped out on the front porch, the north wind chilled her. She waved to Stuart, who approached from the ranch buildings.

"Good morning. I was coming to check on you. Kirby had to leave for several hours, so I'm to look after you today."

"I don't want to take your time, but I would like to talk to the Indians. Is it safe for me to go to their camp?"

"Yes. I'll take you over and introduce you to Sitting Bull. He speaks a little English and will talk to you."

Stuart strolled along slowly and pointed out the various buildings. Not far from the house, they passed the bunkhouse and chuck house built of logs. A large barn adjoined the huge corral, enclosed by a board fence, in which about thirty horses grazed.

A Negro worked in a shed, fueling a forge. Two horses stood, their backs to the wind, waiting for new shoes.

"Mornin', Ike," Stuart called, and the man flashed them a friendly smile.

"Ike used to be the blacksmith at Fort Robinson, but when his enlistment ended, he'd had enough of the army. We were glad to hire him—a ranch this size needs a full-time blacksmith."

They crossed the bridge over a swift-running creek, and Stuart pointed to a row of cabins along the bank of the stream. "That first one is my home."

He opened a wooden gate and walked toward the Indian camp. Sitting Bull stood in front of one of the tepees, and he approached them, limping slightly, hand outstretched in greeting.

"*Hou, cola!*"

The chief wore a dirty white sombrero on his massive head, and twin braids of hair tied with strips of elk skin swung to his waist. He wore a white man's shirt over his broad shoulders, and a blanket wrapped around his tapering middle dragged the ground when he walked. A silver crucifix hung around his neck. Sitting Bull's stern face was pitted with small-pox scars, but the large, curved nose below his brooding eyes seemed the most prominent feature of his visage.

Brenna couldn't believe this was the same man she'd seen a few years ago. Then he'd been dressed in buckskin breeches and a long hunting shirt, with a gaily embroidered war bag slung over his shoulder. He'd worn a warbonnet decorated with two hundred eagle feathers that dragged the floor when he stood up. Life had obviously not gone well for Sitting Bull.

Stuart spoke to the Sioux chief in his own language, and when Sitting Bull's eyes turned toward her, Brenna knew that Stuart had explained her presence. He motioned them inside the lodge, and to Brenna's relief, Stuart went with her.

"You wish to speak to me?" the old man said in halting English.

"I'll interpret, so say what you like," Stuart assured her with a smile.

Brenna explained her mission and ended by saying, "My father had great respect for the Sioux, and he wanted to write a book that told the true story of your people. He said that much of what we read in the East is inaccurate. Please talk to me of your tribe. I will be interested in whatever you say."

Sitting Bull sat for several minutes before he started in a forlorn voice. "The Sioux is a dying race. We sell our land, which *Wakantanka* give us. With other chiefs, I traveled to plead our cause before the White Father, but the government agents do not leave us alone. They raise the price, raise the price, until the Sioux reject my advice and sell their land."

When the chief paused, Stuart explained, "In 1868 the government guaranteed the Sioux a huge reservation north and west of here, but when more settlers moved in, the government tried to buy up the land. Sitting Bull has protested, but last year, when the government finally offered a dollar twenty-five an acre, the temptation was too great, and they sold about ten million acres of Indian territory in western Dakota. The Sioux were given a half section of land for each family, but if history repeats itself, speculators will soon get that away from the Indians, for most of them don't have a head for business."

"*Hoye*," Sitting Bull agreed. "Now they have taken our land, they want no more from us. They cut our rations. Our children are hungry. They die like flies from white man's diseases."

"What kind of diseases?" Brenna asked.

Sitting Bull spread his hands wide, looking at Stuart.

"Measles, whooping cough, flu," Stuart replied. "Many deaths among the Sioux last winter."

Hoping to arouse the old man from his pensive mood, Brenna asked, "Will you tell me something about the Sioux religion?"

"The White Buffalo Calf Maiden brought the sacred pipe to the Indian. She also taught the Sioux seven ways to pray to the Great Spirit, and before she left the Sioux, she promised she would appear again at the end of the world."

Sitting Bull reached for a large pipe lying beside him. Eagle feathers hung from where the wooden stem fit onto the red stone bowl carved in the shape of a buffalo's head.

Cradling the pipe in his arm, he continued, "Two men of the Sans Arc tribe were out hunting one day when they saw a beautiful maiden, dressed in white buckskin. One of the men had evil thoughts about the maiden, and the Great Spirit destroyed him. The other hunter received instructions to return to his people and prepare them for coming of the maiden. Soon she appeared in the village, walking in circular, sunwise fashion. She delivered the sacred pipe, telling the chiefs to treat it in a holy way, saying that no impure man should ever look upon the sacred pipe.

"The Buffalo Calf Maiden taught the Sioux nation many sacred ceremonies. The circle is very important in all our beliefs."

Sitting Bull picked up a stick and drew a crude circle on the ground, making Brenna acutely aware of the small, tattooed circle on her arm.

"The instructions of the buffalo maiden taught us of the rite of purification, the way to our visions, the sun dance, the rite of womanhood, and how to make the sacred pipe. After she finished teaching our fathers, the maiden prepared to leave. The warriors begged her to stay with them, saying that they would care for her, but she said that she must return to her father, the Great Spirit."

All was quiet in the tepee, but outside Brenna heard the stamping of horses and the bawling of cattle as she silently contemplated what the chief had said. Could the Sioux concept of the White Buffalo Calf Maiden be based on the biblical teaching of Christ and His promise to return to earth some day? Brenna had a feeling that as she learned more about the Sioux religious beliefs she would be forced to examine and reflect on her own Christian faith. Too long she'd existed on the doctrine of John Anderson. Perhaps this summer she could learn what she, Brenna Anderson, really believed about God and His purpose for the world.

"And has the Buffalo Calf Maiden returned again?" Brenna prodded.

He slowly shook his head. "No. She sat down and arose again as a young red and brown buffalo calf. She walked farther, rolled over, and became a white buffalo. Soon she turned into a black buffalo. After that she disappeared into the distance and hasn't been seen since. But she will come again, and this time she will not bring the sacred pipe, but perhaps she'll wear around her neck the lost *piedra de toque*."

Brenna jumped and her flesh crawled as a hot flush engulfed her body. *Piedra de toque!* The touchstone!

Brenna staggered to her feet quickly, and Stuart reached out a hand to her. Seeing the surprise on his face, she remembered belatedly that she must not give anyone a hint of her main mission this summer, so she pretended that her pulse wasn't racing full speed and gave Sitting Bull her hand.

"Thank you. I hope that you'll talk with me again before you leave."

Sitting Bull remained seated but inclined his head slightly. She gasped for breath, thinking she couldn't stand the confinement of this tepee any longer and rushed toward the opening. Stuart steadied her with one hand.

"Are you all right?" he inquired anxiously.

"Yes. I suddenly grew very warm and just needed some fresh air."

She opened her cloak and let the strong north wind filter over her skin.

"You should get plenty of it out here," Stuart said dryly as he planted his sombrero more firmly on his head. Brenna didn't like the quizzical look in his gray eyes.

Brenna noticed several Sioux women squatted nearby watching as two Bar-C cowboys headed three steers into the pasture. The steers bolted across the field, and several mounted Indians chased them, shooting at the frightened animals. All three animals tumbled and fell, and the women hurried toward them, carrying knives and containers, followed by a bevy of children.

Brenna's stomach churned as one of the women skinned back a steer's hide and sliced off a chunk of raw meat, which she handed to one of the boys. He started chewing on the bloody meat, and Brenna gagged. Sensing a presence behind her, she encountered Brown's sardonic, amused eyes.

"Tired of Sioux culture already? When you write about the savages eating raw meat, be sure and say that the white man drove them to their uncivilized ways by killing off the buffalo and then cutting rations until the Sioux nation is slowly starving to death."

Her heaving stomach, as well as Brown's attitude, angered Brenna. She lifted her hand to slap him, but he caught her hand before the blow landed. She jerked her hand away, and shoved him aside.

"When I want your comments, I'll ask for them," she said harshly. "Get out of my way."

He stepped aside and gave her an ironic bow as she bolted

from the Indian camp. She didn't heed Stuart's, "Wait a minute," but hurried toward the ranch house.

When Kirby met her on the porch, his welcome smile soothed her ruffled feathers, but with a sinking feeling, she wondered if her plans were doomed for failure. Considering today's experience, her efforts to tackle the Sioux nation might prove as disastrous as Custer's campaign.

4

Only Kirby and Brenna sat down at the long table for lunch. He pulled out a chair and seated her before he took his place. Brenna had difficulty forcing the soup past her mouth, and she noted that Kirby had a puzzled look on his face as he chatted with her.

"Is anything wrong?" he inquired at length. "Didn't you enjoy your visit to Sitting Bull?"

She forced a smile to her face. "Better not ask me about it now, or I'll never finish this bowl of soup. It's delicious, so I don't want to hurt Tatoke's feelings; besides, if I don't eat, Mendy will start pestering me."

Kirby nodded understandably. "One's first encounter with the Sioux can be pretty overwhelming. What are your plans for the afternoon?"

"I want to record the things that Sitting Bull told me. He explained quite a lot about the Sioux religion, and if I don't write it down soon, I may forget something."

"That'll be fine. I want to show you around the Bar C, but we'll leave that until another day. My afternoon's duties might take me farther away then you'd want to ride the first time anyway. That is, unless you're an experienced rider."

Brenna shook her head. "No, I'm not. I've ridden a little, and I'm not afraid of horses, but that's about all the qualifications I have as a horsewoman."

"Oh, well, we'll soon take care of that. I'll have Brown pick out a good mount for you," Kirby assured her as he led the way into the parlor. "Let's sit here awhile. I have a few minutes before I need to leave." After he'd settled her into a comfortable reed chair, he pulled a matching rocker close to her. "Now, tell me what upset you this morning."

Brenna avoided his eyes. She couldn't tell him about Sitting Bull's reference to the touchstone, nor could she reveal her strange fascination with Brown.

"Oh, I suppose I shouldn't have been shocked, but when we left Sitting Bull's tepee, the Indian women were carving up the beef you'd given them. Some of the children ate the beef *raw*, and I'm afraid that turned my stomach."

He laughed sympathetically. "That's enough to upset you. Of course, the Sioux have eaten buffalo meat that way for centuries, and they think nothing of it, but sad to say, the children were probably so hungry they'd have eaten anything. I'm not proud of how our government has treated the Sioux. You'll see many things to distress you as you travel around the reservation, but don't let that ruin your plans."

"Oh, I know. I've heard my father talk about Sioux customs enough to realize that. I'm not usually easily shocked, and I do want to visit the camp again while the Indians are still here."

"Sitting Bull will be eating with us tomorrow night, and you'd best be warned that his table manners wouldn't be acceptable in Philadelphia. I'll not place you near him."

Brenna laughed. "Now that I'm warned, I'll manage. Let's just forget about my foolishness." She knew that she wouldn't forget it, and she wondered what Stuart thought of her strange behavior.

"We're also having other guests tomorrow—some men from Fort Robinson. They want to talk with Sitting Bull about some trouble on the reservation."

Kirby rose with obvious regret. "I enjoy your company, but this ranch won't run itself."

After he left, Brenna's confused thoughts focused on Sitting Bull's words, "When the Buffalo Calf Maiden return, she'll wear around her neck the lost *piedra de toque.*"

Although her Christian faith refuted any thought that the touchstone could have any power, still she couldn't help think that the *piedra de toque* was going to have a tremendous effect on her life.

She grabbed her cloak and ran outside. Blinking her eyes rapidly to adjust to the bright April sun, Brenna wandered aimlessly off the porch, with no destination in mind.

Sounds of the forge indicated that Ike was still shoeing horses, and she moved in that direction. Several Indian children stood around the shed, watching the sparks as Ike hammered the glowing iron and the hissing steam as he deftly inserted the finished product into the water tank. His actions fascinated the children, but the black stallion receiving the shoes didn't like the commotion, and as the sparks flew he tugged at the ropes holding him. With one mighty pull, he freed himself and reared on his hind feet.

The Indian children scattered, except for one small boy, who caught his foot in a rope. With horror Brenna saw that the child would be trampled by the stallion's feet when he landed, for Ike, struggling with the horse, didn't see the child beside him. Quickly Brenna darted into the shed, grabbed the boy by the arm, and jerked with all her strength. His foot came loose, and she and the boy both tumbled to safety in a mudhole.

"Miss, are you hurt?" Ike called, but he had his hands full holding the stallion and couldn't come to help them.

Brenna sat up and found a clean spot on her dress to wipe her hands and the face of the child, who was splattered with grime. Busy working with the boy, who hadn't uttered a word, Brenna didn't know that Brown had hurried to her side until his strong arms lifted her from the ground.

"You all right?" he asked anxiously.

She walked a few steps and in a shaky voice said, "I think so. But what about this little fellow?" The other boys had returned for him, so he broke loose from Brenna's grasp and ran to them. She laughed as the boys raced toward Sitting Bull's camp.

"He must not be hurt, or he couldn't run like that."

Still at her side, Brown said remorsefully, "Should have stayed to help Ike with stallion, but he seemed quiet enough."

"Oh, no harm's done. If the boy hadn't caught his foot in the rope, there wouldn't have been any problem."

"Very brave of you," Brown intoned, and Brenna couldn't look at him. Was it approval she heard in his voice? "I saw how quickly you moved—could have been hurt yourself."

"I probably *will* be hurt when Mendy sees what I've done to these clothes," she joked. Anything to avoid thinking about Brown and how his presence affected her.

Brenna had a few sore spots the next morning but no other reminder of her tumble in the mud. She had slept later than she'd intended to, and Mendy hadn't bothered to awaken her.

Mid-morning she heard Mendy's lumbering steps approaching her room.

"Mistah Brown wants to talk to you, if you got the time."

Brenna didn't want to talk to "Mistah Brown," but she couldn't think of any good reason to say no. He had absented himself from supper the evening before, so again she and Kirby had eaten together and spent the evening alone. She'd come to the conclusion that Brown wished to avoid her, but why had he come this morning?

"Tell him I'll be down in a few minutes."

Entering the parlor quietly, she had a moment to compose herself before Brown turned and spied her. He removed his sombrero and bowed slightly. His eyes always seemed to be masked so that she could never determine his thoughts.

"Kirby told me to find a horse for you. If you have time now, I'll show you what we have and perhaps let you ride some of them around the corral. You could choose which one you like."

"I have the time," she said, not looking directly at him but glancing instead at her dress. "Perhaps I should change into something else. I have a riding outfit."

"Yes, you'd be more comfortable."

"I'll only be a short while." Turning toward the hallway, she stopped abruptly when his hand gripped her arm. His touch seemed to burn through the sleeve of her garment, and she poised like a startled animal, not daring to face him.

"Look at me, Brenna."

Her body shifted toward him, and he dropped his hand from her arm.

"I'm sorry for the way I've acted to you—couldn't believe a beautiful woman like you could be interested in my people. Sometimes my own mixed-up life makes me lash out at others. It's bad being Indian in a white man's world!" He held out his hand. "I'd like to be friends."

Brenna lowered her eyes again, finding it impossible to hold his warm gaze. A friendly Brown would be harder to cope with than an antagonistic one, Brenna reflected, for her pulse accelerated at such a pace that she stepped backward, fearful he would sense her agitation.

But bravely she faced him and reached for his hand. "Yes,

I would like very much to be your friend." He watched her as she quickly mounted the stairs.

The gray tailored riding outfit accented her height, and Brenna knew she looked good in it. Brown's face no longer wore a mask, and admiration lit his face when she again entered the parlor.

He opened the outside door for her, saying, "Not often that I see a woman as tall as me. Your eyes are on a level with mine."

"I don't mind telling you that it's a blamed nuisance to be so tall. In our culture a woman is expected to be delicate, petite, docile. Those characteristics were left out of my make-up."

He gave her a warm smile. The mask had disappeared completely from his face, but his eyes still said things she couldn't interpret. "Don't want to be different. Among our people, you might pass for the Buffalo Calf Maiden. She was a tall woman."

Brenna started. Blast the White Buffalo Calf Maiden—couldn't these Sioux talk about anything else?

"Sitting Bull spoke about her yesterday, but I couldn't understand everything he said, even though Stuart interpreted. You speak English well, and now that we're friends, perhaps you'll be able to explain the Sioux to me."

With a touch of bitterness in his voice, he said, "Oh, yes, I pick up the white man's ways quickly. Too quickly for the good of my soul." He pounded his chest. "I have war inside, the Sioux fighting the white man's culture. I don't know which one will win."

The brisk breeze molded her riding habit to her hips and breast as Brown opened the gate into the corral. His eyes raked her body approvingly. *No white man would look at me so openly. What am I going to do about him?*

She riveted her attention on the three horses tied to the fence. Brown's mask dropped into place, and he imperson-

ally indicated a white-faced brown horse with white sprinkled in her mane.

"This filly is the most comfortable ride we have, but she's
frisky sometimes."

Pointing to the next horse, a piebald, he said, "Pickles is
slow and easy, but she does not have much speed." Patting
the rump of the third horse, a gray mare, he commented,
"And you have no trouble with Two Bits—feels like sitting in
a rocking chair. Want to try them all and take your pick?"

Brenna put her arm around the neck of the brown horse,
who nuzzled her nose on Brenna's arm. "Let me ride this
one first. What's her name?"

"Raindrop." Gathering the reins of all three horses over
one arm, Brown moved toward the building beside the corral. "I'll choose a saddle for you from the tack room. I
thought you'd use Mrs. Chapman's sidesaddle, but seeing as
how you dressed for range life, might as well ride astride."

"Did you know Mrs. Chapman?"

"Yes. My mother came here as housekeeper about ten
years ago. Dove and I came along. We lived in one of the
little houses." He motioned toward two log cabins near the
creek. He gave Brenna a keen glance. "But there was nothing
between Tatoke and Mr. Chapman before his wife died."

"I wasn't suggesting any such thing," Brenna replied
crisply, and Brown grinned at her.

"Now don't get your back up and start spatting with me
again."

She didn't answer but stood admiring his broad shoulders
and smooth movements as he entered the tack room. With
his back to her, she couldn't envision him as an Indian. Even
in his actions, he didn't differ much from Stuart or Kirby,
and it surprised her that he'd shed so much of his native
culture. Even more than Dove had, it seemed, but she
thought of his strange comment about being at war inside. If
that was true, he must spend some miserable moments.

By the time Brenna had ridden all three horses, the insides of her legs and thighs ached. She spraddled when she tried to walk.

"Want to try Raindrop again?"

"Oh, I don't think I can. I'm ashamed to be such a softie."

"You'll get used to it soon. Best thing to do is ride every day. I'll keep all three horses close by, so you can choose which one you want. I'll teach you how to saddle your horse, too. Somebody will be around all of the time, probably, but you still need to learn how to saddle. Feel like going to Sioux camp? Want to show you something."

"I guess so—if we walk slowly."

They crossed the small stream and walked toward Sitting Bull's tepee. Horses grazed at random in the pasture, and Brown stopped beside an old gray horse. He placed his hand beneath the horse's mane, and the animal nickered, knelt on his front legs, raised himself erect, and held out one hoof to Brenna.

She stared in amazement. "Well, of all things! Who taught him to do that?"

"Buffalo Bill."

"You mean the showman?"

"Yes. Sitting Bull traveled with the Wild West Show a few years ago, and Bill gave him this horse when he left the show." Brown patted the back of the horse. "Poor old horse. About like the rest of the Sioux now—not much good."

They walked amicably back toward the house, stepping slowly in deference to Brenna's sore legs. On the porch, she laid her hands on his arm.

"I like being friends, Brown, and I want to explain about yesterday. I'll admit I was shocked to see the children eating the raw meat, but I'd already received a jolt from something Sitting Bull had said."

"Want to tell me what?"

She hesitated and then shook her head. "Not just now."

Brenna ate lunch alone, welcoming the solitude; and the remainder of the afternoon, she rested on the bed. Late evening, when Mendy plodded upstairs, she mumbled, "Company for supper. We got all kinds of work to do."

"I'm sure no one expects you to work, if you'd rather sit around."

"You know I ain't one to sit around. I'm helping."

"Stop complaining then and help me dress."

Mendy looked at her suspiciously. "What've you been doin' to yore face? It looks like a piece of raw meat."

Brenna moved toward the mirror as quickly as her sore joints would let her. For once Mendy hadn't exaggerated, and Brenna groaned.

"Gracious! It must be windburn. The wind blew hard when I rode this afternoon." She lifted her hand to her red face, which felt warm to the touch.

"Don't you worry. I'll fix you up in a hurry," Mendy crooned as she bustled around, gently massaging Brenna's face with soothing creams. In spite of her complaints, Mendy loved to wait on Brenna.

"There you are, almost as good as new. We'll put a little powder around here and there, and you won't even need colorin'."

"I want to wear this red dress." Red had always been her favorite color, and Brenna actually seemed to glow when Mendy dropped the red silk dress over her shoulders. The garment had a bell skirt and high collar edged with lace. The close-fitting sleeves came right above her elbow, with a large cap at the top. Mendy fastened the small, covered buttons, pulling the tight bodice over her breasts.

Brenna looked critically in the mirror for the result. This was one of the first dresses she'd worn without the bulky bustle, and although she felt a bit naked without it, she still liked the way the full skirt fell gracefully from her thin waist.

Searching for some jewelry, her hand touched the leather

bag that contained the touchstone. For a moment she considered wearing it, but thinking of Sitting Bull's presence and his reference to the *piedra de toque*, she laid it aside, choosing instead a strand of her mother's pearls.

Brenna waited in her room until Dove came. The Indian girl hurried into the room just before six o'clock. "Sorry to be late." She stopped. "You're beautiful!"

"Oh, I don't know about that." The comment had pleased her, however. "You look lovely yourself."

Dove wore a white buckskin dress, and her hair hung straight over her shoulders. She bore a great resemblance to the peaceful bird for whom she'd been named; Brenna noted the serenity that shone from Dove's brown eyes and envied her. Dove knew who she was and had accepted her lot in life. *I can never be completely happy until I know, and then I wonder if I'll ever be happy again.*

As they walked together down the wide steps, Brenna said, "I like your dress. Wonder if I could find one like it?"

"Several women on the reservation make them. I'll take your measurements and order one for you."

Sitting Bull sat stiffly in a reed chair, and Stuart squatted beside him, chatting in Sioux. Brown stood by the mantel, and he favored Brenna and his sister with a slight smile.

Kirby rose immediately, saying, "Brenna, Dove, come meet our guests."

Indicating the lanky man in uniform, he said, "This is Colonel Guy V. Henry, with the Ninth Cavalry at Fort Robinson."

Henry's light hair thinned at the temples, and he sported a full mustache. Drooping eyelids gave him a sluggish appearance, but noting the many decorations spread across the chest of his blue uniform, one of which was a medal of honor, Brenna doubted he'd done much sleeping during his career

"It's also a pleasure to have Baptiste Garnier with us tonight. He serves Fort Robinson as scout and interpreter."

Garnier stood several inches shorter than Brenna, and she had to smother a smile as she sized up his garments. He flaunted a wool vest and waistcoat, lavishly embroidered, and matching leggings covered his leather breeches from knees to ankles.

Indicating the women, Kirby said, "Gentlemen, meet our guest, Brenna Anderson, of Philadelphia, and I think you know my sister, White Dove."

Both men politely acknowledged the introductions, but since they seemed ill at ease in her presence, Brenna soon gravitated toward Brown.

Under cover of Kirby's conversation with his guests, she said softly, "What else should I know about them?"

"Henry has charge of Fort Robinson's Negro regiment. He's a Civil War veteran. The other man's normally called 'Little Bat.' He's the son of an Oglala Sioux mother and a French father. Been a scout for the army for twenty years or so."

"Wonder why they came tonight?"

"Want to see Sitting Bull. Army's getting edgy about some happenings on the reservation. No matter what happens, army always blames Sitting Bull."

"What things?"

Before he could answer, Mendy appeared in the doorway. "Dinner is served, Mistah Kirby," she announced.

Seating arrangements pleased Brenna, for she sat to the right of Kirby, with Brown on her right. Sitting Bull slumped in a chair on the other side of Brown, so that kept her from facing him. Dove, too, had hinted that Sitting Bull hadn't adjusted to the white man's social dining habits, and Brenna was relieved she wouldn't have to watch him eat.

Kirby indicated that the seat at the end of the table, opposite him, should be Colonel Henry's. Dove sat to Henry's right, with Little Bat between her and Stuart, who sat down across the table from Brenna. She felt secure, surrounded by these three men she'd come to admire in a few days.

Kirby soon had Colonel Henry talking about his Civil War exploits, and he and Stuart discovered that they'd fought in some of the same battles, albeit on opposing sides. Tatoke and Mendy carried in a platter of steak, bowls of potatoes, fried apples, and stewed tomatoes, as well as a mound of biscuits.

Sitting Bull grunted a time or two, and Brown said nothing except a few polite comments to Brenna, but Stuart and Kirby kept a conversation going with Colonel Henry. Garnier spoke occasionally with Dove, but Brenna kept her eyes on her plate, trying to ignore the slurping sounds that came from Sitting Bull. *You probably won't know how to eat in a Sioux camp either*, she derided herself.

When they returned to the parlor, Brenna sat on the couch between Brown and Stuart. Colonel Henry pulled a chair close to Sitting Bull, who sat, obviously ill at ease, in a rocking chair. They conversed in Sioux, but Brown and Stuart took turns translating, so Brenna followed the general gist of the conversation.

"I've heard that Buffalo Bill has invited you to go on tour with him in Europe next season. Do you plan to go?" Henry asked.

Sitting Bull stolidly shook his head, and Brenna thought Henry seemed relieved.

"It is impossible. My people need me. *Wakantanka* has revealed much to me. The Sioux are doomed. Where once an eagle forecast that I would be leader of my people, a meadowlark say that I will die, and that my own people will kill me." He tore open his shirt, and Brenna gasped at the scars on his chest. Stuart touched her lightly on the hand.

"I, who have sacrificed the scarlet blanket, to be killed by the Sioux! But I will not desert my people. Not even to see the Great Mother Victoria will I leave my people."

"Speaking of sacrificing the scarlet blanket, Major McLaughlin says he's heard rumors that the Sioux at Standing Rock are planning a sun dance, and when he ordered you to stop it, you laughed in his face."

The chief stared at Henry and said bitterly, "The white man has taken our land and the buffalo, why can you not leave us our religion?"

"Because the major also says that the sun dance is not religion but simply a barbarous ritual of torture designed to put a curse on whites."

"Major McLaughlin is a fool."

"Perhaps, but he's also the agent of the United States government on your reservation. It would be well if the two of you could get along."

"Sitting Bull does not pick a fight with any man."

"Concerning the sun dance, isn't it true that when you took part in one and shed the scarlet blanket you just mentioned, that you made the medicine that defeated General Custer?"

The Sioux chief fixed Henry with a sardonic stare. "*You* believe that—believe that a savage's sacrifice to the Great Spirit could defeat the pony soldiers?"

Henry's face turned red, and with difficulty he bit back an angry reply. "We're getting away from the main point. I'm asking you to comply with McLaughlin's request and not to have a sun dance."

"Sitting Bull does not *have* sun dances. It is the Sioux's way of sacrificing to the Great Spirit for unity among our people, as instructed by the White Buffalo Calf Maiden. It is no different from the white man's religion, except once a Sioux is purified by *Wakantanka*, he does not lie and steal and kill. The white man's religion does not teach these things, for not one promise have they kept to the Sioux. I repeat, why can you not leave us our religion?" Majestically, he stood, nodded to Kirby, and strode out the door.

A tense silence gripped the room's occupants after the chief's dramatic departure.

Colonel Henry broke it with an apologetic laugh. "I told Colonel Tilford that it wouldn't do any good to talk to him." And he added, "I agree with the old man. Why can't we leave them something?"

"I thought the government ordered a halt to sun dances when they herded all the Sioux on reservations?" Kirby said.

"That's what McLaughlin thought, too, but he's been hearing rumors lately."

"They have never completely stopped the sun dance, for it's life and light to the Sioux," Little Bat said. "The sun dance is as important to the Sioux as Easter is to the white man's religion. My advice is to let them have their sun dance."

"That's my opinion, too," Stuart said. "I've seen a few sun dances, and no one is required to go through the torture ritual. It's a voluntary act between the brave and the Great Spirit. If the colonel wants to worry about something, he'd better give some thought to the ghost dance."

Little Bat nodded sagely, and Henry asked, "Ghost dance? What's that?"

"I'm not sure," Stuart said, "but I've heard some murmurings about it."

"I heard something last week at Pine Ridge," Dove said. "A Paiute, beyond the mountains, claims he is the messiah, and he teaches a new religion that is supposed to bring back the buffalo and our dead ancestors, but the white man will be destroyed." Colonel Henry stared at her in amazement as she added, "But not many pay any attention to it."

"Let's hope not." Henry dismissed the matter and turned to Brenna. "I trust you haven't chosen a bad time to pay us a visit. How long do you intend to stay?"

"Perhaps until I wear out my welcome." Seriously, she added, "Probably I'll leave before summer is over."

"Then let me invite you to visit us at Fort Robinson. We have monthly entertainments and dances. Perhaps you will bring her to the one next week, Kirby."

"It will be my pleasure."

Walking upstairs with Dove that night, Brenna said, "Don't you find it a problem to mix your Christian training with the practices of the Sioux?"

"A little. I'm Christian, but don't see anything wrong with the sun dance. Our *Wakantanka* is same as white man's God. Indians just don't know about Jesus as Savior. I try to tell them."

"Did the missionaries bring the message of *Wakantanka?*"

"No, long before that. I believe the story of the White Buffalo Calf Maiden is the same as the second coming of Jesus. I don't know how Sioux got mixed up."

5

The next morning not a sign of the Sioux camp remained in the pasture, and Brenna wondered if Sitting Bull had hastened his departure because he didn't like Colonel Henry's veiled warnings. Since she awakened early, Brenna sat up in bed, pulled the covers around her, and filled several pages of her notebook with the information she'd learned the night before.

"I'm glad the Injuns are gone," Mendy commented, when she came to help Brenna dress.

"You'll have to get used to them. In a few weeks, I'm planning to spend some time on the Sioux reservation. I suppose you'll want to go, too."

"Miss Brenna, you just got to be jokin'."

"No, I mean it. I heard last night about a new ghost dance some of the Indians are performing. I thought I should see it for myself."

Mendy stopped brushing Brenna's hair, and in the mirror Brenna saw her widened eyes.

"You mean ghosts a-dancin' around?"

"That's what it sounds like."

"All a bunch of lies, I'll bet. I don't believe in ghosts." Mendy's hands shook as she continued brushing.

"No, I don't either—probably not even called a ghost dance."

Mendy cast her eyes heavenward. "O Lord, why'd You ever let us come to this country?"

"Why, I supposed you were having a good time. I hear tell you've been eyeing that cowboy Ike, who works for Kirby."

Drawing herself up indignantly, Mendy retorted, "There ain't a word of truth in that. Not that I couldn't if I wanted to. I want you to know that I got funds of my own—you can't order *me* around." She flounced out of the room, to the sound of Brenna's laughter, but she stuck her head back in before she closed the door. "And I ain't goin' to any Injun reservation."

She slammed the door, and Brenna remarked aloud, "I accomplished that without too much trouble. I wondered how I could keep her from following me around all summer."

Dove soon knocked on the door and entered at Brenna's call.

"Would you like to go riding this morning?"

"That sounds like fun, but I'll warn you, I don't do so well on horseback. I'm still sore from riding around the corral yesterday."

"You'll soon get used to it. Dress warmly though. Cold wind from northwest today."

"You're right about the wind," Brenna agreed as they stepped off the porch and headed toward the ranch buildings.

"No very warm weather here until May. Good idea for you to stay at the ranch for a few more weeks. Life on our reservation's not so good this time of year."

A large crowd had gathered around the corral, and Dove laughed slightly. "I wondered where everyone went to this morning. Must be something exciting going on. Only two things could cause so many men to be out on a Sunday morning—a fight or a new horse in the remuda."

Kirby perched atop the high fence, but he jumped down when he saw them.

"I thought I'd take Brenna riding this morning—show her around the ranch a bit," Dove said.

"Great idea. But come watch the bronco busting first."

"So it's a new horse!"

"Two of them," Kirby said. "Sitting Bull brought along two that were too wild for the Sioux braves. Brown thought they'd be all right, so I bought them."

Brenna moved close to the corral and peered through the wooden bars. A piebald horse, tied to the gate, stomped his feet and tugged at the rope, the muscles in his back in perpetual motion. He shook his head angrily, apparently trying to rid himself of a blindfold.

Ike stood at his head, trying to hold him. The horse kicked out with his front feet, and the cowboy jumped backward, narrowly missing an injury. Brown sat on the gate, whistling tonelessly, speculatively studying the animal's movements.

"Saddle him, Ike, and I'll try him out."

"Sakes, Mistah Brown, I can't even hold his head. Somebody else'll have to put on the saddle."

Stuart climbed over the fence and slid cautiously into the corral, with a saddle over his arm. He slapped the saddle on the animal's back and jumped aside as the horse reared, knocking Ike against the fence and throwing the saddle into the air.

"Better not try it, Brown," Kirby cautioned. "Let him get used to being on the ranch with the other horses. He looks like a killer to me."

"He just thinks he's a killer. If he doesn't like a saddle, I'll ride him bareback."

"No, Brown," Dove called, and he turned, seeing the two women. Brenna wanted to add her protests, but she could tell by looking at him that they might as well save their breath. He'd ride the horse if it killed him. She wondered then, if once he set his mind to something, anyone could change it.

Today Brown had shed the cowboy's trappings. Naked from the waist up, he wore buckskin trousers and moccasins.

"Hold him, Stuart, till I get on his back, then turn him loose when I say."

He gingerly lowered himself onto the heaving back of the horse. Every muscle of the piebald's body quivered in anger as the man slipped astride him, but otherwise he didn't move. Brown wrapped his arms around the horse's neck and clamped his legs under its belly.

In a low voice, he said, "Okay, Stuart. Ready."

What happened next was almost too quick for Brenna to follow. Stuart cut the ropes that held the animal, Brown jerked off the blindfold, and the horse galvanized into action. He reared into the air, trying to rid his back of the hated human, but Brown held on. Then the piebald bolted across the corral, slamming into the fence, where a number of cowboys watched. They rolled backwards off the fence at the onslaught. Still Brown stayed on the animal.

Brown's performance fascinated Brenna as much as the piebald's antics. The long, smooth muscles in Brown's back moved as evenly as the pistons of a well-oiled machine. His lips parted into a smile, and she shuddered at the violent and explosive recklessness he displayed. He actually enjoyed the struggle with the horse.

The piebald stiffened his legs, walked jerkily around the enclosure, then reared several more times, and with his body swaying, he jumped into the air.

"Watch out, Brown, he's falling," Kirby called frantically as he climbed the fence.

The piebald slumped to his side and started to roll, but just before he hit the earth, Brown pulled his legs free and landed on his feet, running. The fall stunned the horse, and Brown reached the safety of the fence before the horse lunged to his feet and looked around for his prey. Head down, the animal pawed the ground and raced around the corral.

Blood oozed from Brown's nose, and sweat glistened on his brown torso, but he seemed heedless of his own discomfort. A mocking smile spread across his face. "Playful, ain't he? Rope him, Stuart, and I'll try him again."

"Oh, please don't ride him anymore," Brenna surprised herself by saying. She handed Brown her handkerchief, and with an ironic gleam in his eyes, he accepted the cloth and wiped his face.

"That's what I'm paid to do around here, Miss Brenna. Have to earn my keep."

She turned away from him and said to Dove, "If he wants to kill himself, I'm not going to stay and watch. I'll be at the house when you're ready to go riding."

Her legs trembled as she walked away from the corral, and she leaned against the stable, nausea gripping her. Why did Brown flaunt danger so readily? Didn't life mean anything to him?

Shouts from the corral drew her attention, and against her will, she hurried back to watch. This time they'd put a hackamore over the horse's head, and Brown had changed his moccasins for spurred boots. The horse tried to repeat all his former tricks, but apparently he'd met his master, for after long minutes of grueling punishment to Brown's body, the horse stopped dead in his tracks and walked meekly where Brown directed him. Brenna hastened away from the fence and Dove followed.

"Brown hasn't yet found a horse he can't master," Dove said, pride in her voice.

"One of these days he may not be so lucky. That horse nearly killed him."

"Not luck. He understands horses—knows what they're going to do before they strike." Stopping at the stable, she said, "What horse do you want?"

"The one Brown called Pickles. After what I've seen this morning, I don't want a frisky horse."

In an hour they circled the ranch headquarters, and Brenna had some comprehension of the extent of the Bar C. The ranch was characterized by a rolling short-grass prairie laced with a wide creek. From a wide mesa, about five miles from the house, they could see long distances in every direction. To the west were outcroppings of ancient muds and shales. Southward, the prairie extended indefinitely, and herds of pronghorn antelope grazed contentedly on the new spring grass. To their north, the prairies gave way to rugged sandstone buttes that formed the backbone of pine-covered ridges.

"What beautiful scenery!" Brenna exclaimed. "Sure would be a good place for a house."

"Too windy, for one thing, and it's a sacred spot for the Sioux, so the Chapmans have never changed it."

"Sacred? How?"

"The young Sioux come sometimes to commune with the Great Spirit, asking for a vision. Sioux call it *Wakantepee*—in English it means Spirit House."

"Dove, many things of your religion are beautiful. Tell me more about it. Does the boy come alone?"

"Yes, he comes to plead with the Great Spirit for a filling of supernatural power. Varies from tribe to tribe, but among my people, the Miniconjou, a boy first purifies mind and body by passing through pine-needle smoke. Goes to a hilltop, and stays for days, fasting, praying to the Great Spirit. Vision may have different meanings. Boy makes medicine bundle to contain things related to the vision."

Brenna thought of the leather bag she'd found in her father's trunk. Could that have been some Sioux's "medicine bundle"?

"Did Brown do this when he was a boy?"

"Yes. After we moved to Bar C. He came here to *Wakante-pee* and stayed for three days."

Hesitantly, Brenna said, "I don't know how you can believe this. Isn't it inconsistent with your Christian faith?"

"Oh, I don't think so. Sioux religion's pretty much like Christianity, except. . . ."

"Except there is no belief in Jesus Christ and that He died for our sins," Brenna finished for her.

"Yes, I believe in Him, but not many Sioux do."

"My dad often talked about the similarities between the beliefs of the native Americans and Christianity. He sometimes wondered, if long before the coming of the Spanish, there hadn't been people here from Europe or Asia to evangelize the Indians."

"Maybe, but I think the Great Spirit revealed truth to my people."

"Remember what is recorded in Hebrews, 'God, who at sundry times and in divers manners spake in time past unto the fathers by the prophets, Hath in these last days spoken unto us by his Son. . . .' "

"Yes, I know, but it's hard to convince Sioux," Dove said as she spurred her horse to greater speed. "We must hurry. Kirby has worship services each Sunday before dinner."

In late afternoon, after the service, Brenna noticed some cowboys hazing a herd of cattle into the big enclosure where Sitting Bull's camp had been.

"Tomorrow is the day for the beef ration," Dove explained.

"Beef ration?"

"Yes, since buffalo are almost gone, the government provides beef for reservation Indians, and Kirby has the contract for the Pine Ridge Agency. The men deliver animals twice each month, and they'll leave about daybreak in the morning to take the cattle."

At supper, Kirby said, "Everybody has had a chance to entertain you except me. Tomorrow is my day. I'm going to take you to the beef hunt."

"Oh, Kirby, I don't think she'll like it," Dove objected.

"She wants to learn about the Sioux culture. She may as well see everything."

"I want to go," Brenna said. "I don't have to ride horseback, though, do I? That little jaunt with Dove about did me in."

"No, we'll go in the buckboard. We can leave several hours after the herd does and get there in time."

"Tell me about the beef ration."

"It's a matter of necessity for the tribes," Kirby explained. "The buffalo provided a complete livelihood for the Plains Indians, and when the whites killed off the big herds, the government began to furnish cattle, but it's a poor substitute for the buffalo herds, especially now that the rations have been cut. At first, the government guaranteed each Indian over seven hundred pounds of beef annually, but last year that was reduced considerably."

"Still sounds like a lot of meat to me."

"But it cut down our ranch income," Kirby said with a laugh.

"I seem to remember Dad talking about it, or maybe I read it in his notes. Isn't there opposition to this beef ration?"

Dove nodded sagely. "Not the beef ration, but the way it's handled."

"It does create quite a rumpus," Kirby admitted, "but the Sioux insist on 'hunting' the cows. People in the East don't understand that when the Indians kill the cattle themselves, it reminds them of long-ago buffalo hunting."

"Far cry from the buffalo hunts, from what the old men of

the tribe tell," Brown added, "and Stuart says so, too. He's been on a few hunts himself."

"I still want to go."

"Kirby," Brenna said the next morning as they drove to the beef hunt, "I've wondered about something. Seems to me your attitude toward the Indians is a lot different from that of the few other whites I've met around here."

"What do you mean?"

"Accepting Dove and Brown as family members, having Sitting Bull at the table, eating with you. I think it's wonderful, and the way it should be, but I don't believe very many people are that way."

"It may be more common than you think, but as far as I'm concerned, I'm simply doing what my father did before me. Now Mother was never comfortable with Indians on an equal basis. She entertained anyone Dad brought to the house, but she didn't like it."

They drove a few miles in silence, and then Kirby continued. "You see, when Dad and Stuart came into this country, the Sioux were mighty nice to them. Dad told me lots of times about how a squaw, Tatoke's grandmother, nursed him through a serious illness. In those early days, when he didn't have any money to hire cowboys, the Indians helped him herd the cattle—especially during blizzards. He said, time and again, when he thought his herd had been destroyed, as the weather cleared, Indian braves would show up with some of his cattle they'd watched over during the bad spell."

"But even at that, I'm surprised that you accept Brown and Dove as equals. Apparently you didn't resent your dad's second marriage."

"Why should I?" he said, shrugging his shoulders. "Dad was really good to my mother, but once she was gone, he couldn't do anything more for her. Tatoke had been with

Mother for several years, and she knew our ways, but she never took to them. Even after Dad married her, she continued to do the cooking, wait on the table, but she wouldn't sit down with us. It irritated Dad, but he couldn't change her. Going to school at Carlisle changed Dove and Brown." He gave her a keen look. "Does having them at the table bother you?"

"Oh, no."

They caught up with the cattle about noon. Kirby passed them with a wave of his hand, and soon afterward the buildings of the Pine Ridge Agency came into view. Brenna went with Kirby into the trading post, and while he arranged the cattle sale with the agent, Colonel Royer, Brenna wandered around. The stale smell of cattle hides offended her nose, but she looked with interest at the items on the shelves—iron pots and skillets, stacks of woolen blankets, bolts of colorful calico, and lengths of muslin.

She went outside to see if she could spot Dove's school, which wasn't far away, a small two-room affair. Dove waved from the yard, where she watched the children at play. Kirby soon joined Brenna, and they traveled the few miles south, where tepees dotted the area, and hundreds of Indians stood near a fenced corral, awaiting the arrival of the cattle.

Stuart rode ahead of the cows, and he reined his horse close to the buckboard while the cowboys drove the cattle into a large corral. Armed with bows and arrows, young boys stood near the corral gates, and mounted Indians gathered farther away from the corral, holding knives, pistols, and rifles.

The cowboys released two or three steers at a time and drove them out of the gates. The boys showered them with arrows, and the crazed steers bolted across the prairie, where the Indians on horseback took up the chase. Brenna watched, stupefied, as this procedure occurred time and again.

In less than an hour, dead steers littered the prairie, and

the Sioux women rushed to butcher the carcasses where they had fallen. The cowboys turned homeward, and Kirby guided the buckboard behind them. Brenna stared straight ahead—she hadn't said a word during the beef hunt.

With raised eyebrows, Kirby glanced at Brenna. "Well?" he said.

Brenna's face felt so rigid she thought it would break if she opened her mouth. "That's the most barbaric thing I've ever seen in my life."

"I guess Dove was right," Kirby conceded, "I should have left you at home."

"Those poor animals—to be slaughtered like that."

"I can't see that it's any different than shooting one at a time. Before there's steak, an animal has to be killed. I bet you've eaten beef all your life without giving it a thought."

"That's not the point. You're contributing to the savage ways of the Indians, when the government's trying to civilize them and turn them to white man's ways. They should provide the beef through butcher shops. At least it would be more sanitary than having the animals slaughtered out there in the dirt."

"Listen, Brenna," Kirby countered. "I don't suppose I can make you understand, but I'll try. One of the greatest events in the life of the Plains Indians was the buffalo hunt. The big herds are gone now, and the government has substituted cattle. Maybe it's just letting the Indians down easy, but when they can kill their own cattle even in such a simple way as this, it gives them a little reminder of what they've lost."

"I still think it's a horrible way to treat animals."

"But you're out here to research Indian culture, aren't you? Try to see their side of the situation."

Did she really want to find out that her heritage included Indian ancestors? Sometimes Brenna felt like forsaking it all.

"I'm sorry you're disturbed about this," Kirby finally commented, breaking the silence, "and you're not alone in your feelings. There's much talk of forcing us to do away with the beef hunt, as some members on the board of commissioners consider this a wasteful practice. That really isn't the case, for the Indians use all of the animals just the way they did the buffalo. Even the skins are saved and used for exchange at the trading post. Indians aren't wasters; it isn't part of their culture."

"Then you think this practice will stop soon?"

"Yes, even though the Sioux themselves prefer this method of issue. Besides if we provide beef through butcher shops, it will be a big expense for the government to provide facilities for slaughtering and storage."

It would be one more step in the government's move to force the Sioux toward white man's ways, Brenna thought. As a student of Indian culture, should she want that?

With Dove away during the week, Brenna looked forward to the dance at Fort Robinson. Both Stuart and Kirby insisted that she couldn't start traveling around the country until the weather stabilized, and she was still too soft anyway. Daily rides of a few miles had toughened her, but she hadn't yet developed the stamina of an accomplished horsewoman.

Brenna spent many hours in her room alone, where she tried to sort out her emotions. She'd easily adjusted to life at the Bar C. The girlhood affections she'd harbored for Kirby soon developed into a high regard, but could it be *love*? The real, live Kirby far surpassed the man she'd held in her dreams. A gentleman in all respects, he made her feel wanted, special, and precious.

If she hadn't encountered Brown, life would be much simpler. He'd appeared at the door the day after an unseasonable snowstorm. "Going to town after the mail. Want to come along?" He motioned outside to a sleigh hitched to one of Kirby's buckboard horses.

"Wait until I put on a cloak."

A brilliant sun glistened on the melting snow. Brown bundled her into the sleigh, wrapped a buffalo robe around her, jumped in, and picked up the reins. The sleigh slid away over the snow, and Brenna laughed joyfully.

"I haven't been on a sleigh ride for years. Dad used to own a sleigh, but a few years ago he sold his horses and used public transportation to go to work."

"Makes me feel like walking on snowshoes. Way I traveled in snow as a boy. Hunted rabbits that way."

"Do you miss living on the reservation?"

Pleasure left Brown's face, and his eyes clouded, making Brenna sorry she'd asked.

"Don't answer that. When you think, you're sad. I want to have fun today."

He smiled at her and touched the horse's rump with a whip. The sleigh's speed accelerated, and in a short time they reached Crawford.

"Let's go inside Enderley's drugstore and have some hot chocolate. I see the smoke of the train long way off. Be about an hour before we can leave for home."

The proprietor greeted her warmly enough, but Brenna sensed he wasn't too happy to have Brown sitting at the small table with her. Brown must have been aware of it, too, for his eyes glittered ominously, but the two of them stayed in the warm room until the train's whistle announced its arrival.

"Let's go," Brown said. "If we're there, he'll sort our mail first."

He was right, and they soon climbed into the sleigh to start homeward, but an hour out of Crawford, the sorrel started limping, and Brown stopped the sleigh.

"Must have picked up something in town," he said as he helped Brenna from the vehicle. "Better to stand, until I see what's the matter."

He lifted up the horse's rear foot and pried a chunk of

frozen snow from beneath the shoe. "No wonder you limped. A piece of rock in that snow."

While Brown worked, Brenna picked up a handful of snow, and when he straightened, she blasted him full in the face with the white stuff. Momentarily he stared at her in surprise; then he reached for her, and she bolted away from him across the snow. She could hear him chasing her, and though she ran as fast as possible, he soon grabbed her arm.

"So you want to play!" he said as he sprinkled snow over her head. She laughed and tried to pull away from him, and in the struggle, Brown stepped on her cloak, and they tumbled to the ground.

Brenna's face was buried in the snow, with Brown's heavy body atop her. She turned until her face grazed his, and his arms encircled her shoulders. She couldn't have moved even if she'd wanted to. He lowered his lips to hers, and after a few tantalizing moments, she squirmed in his arms. Brown released her, but she put her arms around his neck and pulled him toward her again.

With a shout, Brown jumped to his feet, and ran toward the unattended horse, now racing for the Bar C, pulling the empty sleigh. The horse had too much of a head start, and Brown came back to pull Brenna to her feet.

"Sorry. Lost my senses, but a long walk home will cool us off. Forget it happened, please."

"It was my fault. I started it." She couldn't look at him, couldn't let him know how his caress had affected her.

Brown took her hand. "Let's go."

More than once in the next hour, he laughingly pulled Brenna out of drifts, but she decided the forced gaiety cloaked more primitive emotions. When they looked up to see the sleigh returning, Stuart was driving, with an extra horse tied to the sleigh. He looked at them incredulously.

"Kinda cool for a stroll, ain't it? What happened?"

Brown bundled Brenna into the sleigh and vaulted into the saddle of the extra horse.

"Sorrel had a gob of snow under his shoe. Stopped to take it out, and he got away from me."

Stuart looked at them suspiciously. "You look as if you've been rolling in the snow."

Brenna self-consciously brushed the snow from her cloak. "We fell into some drifts when we started walking," she said quickly.

"Hmmph!" Stuart mumbled and started the sleigh homeward. In spite of the cold wind, Brenna burned inside. *Why did this have to happen?* she moaned mentally. *Why has my life suddenly become so complicated?* But in her heart she knew that her life would never have been complete if she'd never experienced the sensations Brown aroused in her. She'd never been particularly fond of snow before, but never again would she see a snowflake without remembering Brown.

6

*H*ow could she look forward to going to a dance with Kirby after the sensational experience she'd enjoyed with Brown? Brenna fretted the rest of the week. What had Kirby suspected about the sleigh ride to Crawford?

Surely something must have shown in their faces. No, not in *their* faces, she amended in her thoughts, for Brown's masked eyes didn't reveal one hint of the emotion that had gripped them. But all during that evening, Brenna detected a trace of reproach in Kirby's attitude. Perhaps a guilty conscience made her extra sensitive, though, for the next day Kirby seemed as natural as ever.

Could she be falling in love with two men? Was she in love at all? She couldn't talk it over with Dove, because of the family connections, and if she said anything to Mendy, she'd simply be in for a lecture. Best keep her own counsel.

Brenna decided to wear a sleeveless pink taffeta with the bell-shaped skirt to the dance. Again she rejected the touchstone, choosing instead Susan Anderson's diamond jewelry.

Mendy brushed Brenna's thick hair until it shone, then

coiled it on top of her head. Glancing in the mirror, she noted streaks of brightness darting from her diamond jewelry, and her eyes smoldered like dark velvet.

Dinner would be served in the mess hall, and Kirby had told her to be ready to leave at five o'clock. With a fluttering pulse, she descended the stairs five minutes early. Brown leaned on the fireplace in his favorite stance, but his veiled eyes gave no indication of how her finery impressed him. She switched her gaze away from his quickly. The tension between them for the past few days had been stifling. Brown rarely came to the house, and when he did, he said very little to her.

"Brenna, you're beautiful!" Kirby said. "You make me proud to be your escort, but I'm afraid to take you to the fort. There are too many eligible bachelors there, and I might lose you."

Her face flushed slightly. "I doubt that," she answered, smiling to cover her confusion and wishing he hadn't spoken like that in Brown's presence.

Kirby took the long cloak and draped it around her shoulders, his hands lingering overmuch, she thought. Brenna kept her eyes averted from Brown as they left the room.

The mess hall seemed already crowded when they arrived. Colonel Henry came to them at once, took Brenna's arm and led her around the room, introducing her to the few women there. Several other civilians from Crawford were present, too, so the military didn't completely overwhelm Brenna.

At dinner, she sat between Colonel Henry and Kirby. The linen-covered tables, set with fine china, silver, and crystal, reminded her of the elegant hotels she'd visited in Philadelphia. Subdued light from the shaded oil lamps hanging from the ceiling softened the room's smoky plastered walls and rough wooden floors.

"What a display of finery," Brenna said to Colonel Henry. "I'm impressed as well as surprised."

"Well, our dear ladies give up so much to come to this out-of-the-way place that we like to make things as pleasant as possible for them."

"You've certainly done so. This is a fine meal," she said, taking note of the array of fresh fruits and vegetables that were being placed on the table. "Not that I've been missing anything out here," she hastened to add, "for living at the Bar C is luxury itself."

Kirby cast a grateful glance in her direction.

"Right you are," Henry agreed. "Kirby is an excellent host."

After the leisurely six-course meal, the white-coated waiters cleared the food away and pushed the tables to one corner, while an army band took positions on a small platform. Kirby claimed Brenna for the first dance, skillfully fobbing off the rush of enlisted men.

"The first one is mine, boys, and I'm going to be selfish the rest of the evening, too. I'll share her some of the time."

As his arms went around her for a waltz, Kirby apologized, "I'm not much of a dancer, but I think I can stay off your feet."

"You're doing fine," Brenna said. "Just relax and swing to the feel of the music. I haven't danced much either, although that's one of the things they taught me at school."

By midnight, Brenna thought that she must have danced with every man on the post. Her legs had been numb for a long time, and occasionally she glanced down to be sure she had feet left. When Kirby came for the final dance, she wanted nothing more than to sit down or go home.

"How does it feel to be the belle of the ball?" he asked as the band started playing Schubert's "Serenade."

"Great, since it hasn't happened before. But pleasure has

its price. I may never be able to walk again," she murmured as she leaned against him.

He laughed sympathetically. "Let's thank Colonel Henry for the invitation and leave right away. We could have gone earlier, but I didn't want to spoil your good time."

When the buckboard had cleared the Fort Robinson compound, Kirby put his arm around her and drew her close. She was content in his embrace, for he seemed to represent serenity and security.

"Tired?" he asked.

"Uh-huh . . . but happy too. Thanks for a great evening, Kirby."

"Oh, we'll have many more of these."

When they arrived at the Bar C, he lifted her from the buckboard and carried her to the veranda. "Wait in the parlor until I stable the horses. I won't be long."

When he entered the room, Kirby brought a draft of cold air, and she wrapped herself more closely in the cloak. He took her hands.

"I won't keep you long for I know you're tired, and the room is cold, but I have to tell you that your presence here is the best thing that's ever happened to me. After I met you in Philadelphia, I thought of you often and hoped someday to meet you again. Until you came, I didn't know how lonely I'd been. You've made this house a home again. And I hope someday soon you'll consent. . . ."

Brenna put her hand over his lips to halt the words. "Please, Kirby, don't say it. I don't know how I feel about you yet, and you've been such a dear friend to me that I don't want to hurt you. Just go on being my friend for the time being."

Disappointment spread across his face, but he nodded understandingly. "Forgive me. I know I'm moving too fast. I'll be what you want me to, my dear Brenna, but I'll not do it patiently. I won't keep you longer, but may I at least kiss you good night?"

She lifted her face, trying to blot out the memory of Brown's spontaneous kiss. Kirby's strong lips moved gently over her mouth, and she returned his kiss—ardor for ardor. His touch represented security, peace, love, so why did she have to remember that violent awakening she'd experienced when Brown had kissed her?

When Kirby released her, Brenna lifted her hand to his face and patted it tenderly. "Thanks for understanding and for a great evening. I'll remember this night always."

Conscious that his eyes followed her as she went up the staircase, she didn't look back. She struggled out of her clothes and collapsed on the bed, where she lay awake the rest of the night.

Wanting to avoid both Brown and Kirby, Brenna breakfasted in her room, then dressed in a brown suit and heavy shoes. She took off on foot.

Traveling eastward from the house for about an hour, she came to a knoll that overlooked the Bar C. Here she felt perfectly safe, for she was in sight of the ranch buildings yet isolated.

Sitting on a shale outcropping, her mind seemed to go almost blank, although she'd come here to think. *Kirby or Brown? Kirby or Brown?* kept rolling through her head. In spite of her desire to be alone, when she first saw Stuart riding toward her, she was glad to see him.

"Enjoying your own company, or might I join you for a spell?"

"No, get down, but I can assure you that my company is none too good right now. What've you been doing?" she asked.

He stepped out of the saddle and hunkered down near her.

"Checking out the pastures to see how soon we can turn

the critters out. We've fed hay all winter, and our supply is about gone. How'd you like the dance last night?"

"Fine, but my feet are suffering today."

"Kirby told me that you did lots of dancing and had a good evening, so I'm surprised to find you looking so down-in-the-mouth today."

"I should never have come out here, Stuart. It's brought me nothing but problems."

"How so? I think you fit in right well."

"I'm beginning to lose sight of what I came out here to do."

"You mean to get information about the Sioux to finish your father's book?"

She hesitated a bit, wondering if Stuart could help her find her ancestors, but she said instead, "Things are getting complicated."

"How so?" he quizzed again.

"Do you think it's possible to be in love with two men?"

"Kirby and Brown?" He grinned sympathetically.

She nodded slowly. "Please don't give me away, but I have to talk to someone, and for some reason, I find it easy to talk to you." She surprised a look of pleasure on his face, which disappeared when he caught her glance. "I've never taken much interest in men, but in a month's time, I've become as conscious of those two as a honeybee is of a flower. If it were only *one* of them, I could understand, but how I can be interested in *both* of them is beyond my comprehension."

"They're both good men. It isn't unusual that you'd be attracted to them."

Her eyes narrowed, and she glanced away. "You don't seem to be shocked that I'd be interested in a Sioux. You must have Kirby's kind of tolerance."

He glanced sharply at her and with a slight smile said, "Don't you know that I was married to a Sioux?"

"Why, no!" she gasped. "I'd heard it mentioned that you'd

been married once. You mean she lived here on the ranch with you?"

"Yes, for several years. She was a faithful wife, and I loved her, although that didn't enter into our relationship at first."

"Then are you saying that if I ever have to choose between these two men that Brown would be a good choice?"

"No, I'm not saying any such thing," Stuart stated hurriedly. "In fact, I'd advise you to forget about him. If Kirby wants to marry you, for your own good, I hope you'll say yes."

"But I thought you liked Brown."

"I *do* like him, but you couldn't find happiness with him. Brown is an Indian. No matter how much he dresses like the whites, sits at their table, speaks their language, he's a Sioux, and I expect him to go back to the blanket."

"What does that mean?"

"One of these days, he'll return to the reservation and live like a Sioux."

"He told me he was at war inside."

"No doubt about it. He likes the white man's ways and hates himself because he does. My wife was the same way. Two or three times a year, she'd go back to the tribe, live in a tepee, become full Sioux again. When she was dying, she made me promise to take her body back to the Sioux for tribal burial." He looked off into the distance, and she wondered if he was even conscious of the herd of antelope grazing a few miles away. "You can take them out of the tribe, but you can't take the tribe out of them. It will require generations to civilize the Indians, and I'm not sure they'll be any better off. The Sioux's way of life when I came into this country was hard to beat."

"You think the work at Carlisle is a waste?"

"The school, you mean? No, I don't think it's a waste, for whether or not they like it, the Sioux have to adopt our ways, but it doesn't change their souls—the Indian part of them."

"Speaking of their souls, their religion bothers me, too. All of this talk about the Buffalo Calf Maiden and her return. That's heathenish."

"Yeah. I noticed your reaction to Sitting Bull's narrative that day, but the missionaries have been active among the Plains tribes. There are many Christian Indians."

"I suppose I shouldn't be worrying about Brown and his culture. In a few months, I'll pack up my things and go home and forget I ever knew these two men."

"I doubt that. But as far as Brown is concerned, I don't think he'll ever ask for you. He knows himself and the problems you'd have as his wife, so there's no need to worry about that. But as for Kirby, if you get a chance, take him. I've known him all his life—you couldn't find a better man."

"I'm very fond of him, and to be honest, one of the reasons I came west was to see him again. I've thought about him a lot since he came to our house a few years ago. I anticipated renewing the acquaintance, but the minute I laid eyes on him, there was Brown to complicate things."

Stuart stood and put his hand on the saddle horn. "You'll have to listen to your heart, little gal. What does it tell you to do?"

Dreamily, Brenna replied, "When I'm with Kirby, I feel peaceful, serene, wanted, and cosseted, but Brown is excitement, laughter, desire, and fulfillment, all rolled into one."

Stuart gracefully stepped into the saddle. "I'm sorry to hear that. It's too bad one person can't give you all those things, but think before you leap. I don't want you to be hurt."

"Oh, I don't think I will be," Brenna said. "In a couple of months, I'll board a train and head for Philadelphia, and all this will become a fond memory."

"I hope not. You belong at the Bar C, but it's your decision."

*   *   *

After a few more days passed, and Brown still made no move to see her alone, Brenna accosted him one evening, in front of Stuart and Kirby.

"Brown, I think I've graduated from Pickles. How about going riding with me tomorrow and letting me try out Raindrop?"

The mask lifted momentarily, and Brenna detected a look of surprise. He hesitated perceptibly, and she thought, *Surely he won't turn me down in front of Stuart and Kirby.*

"Can't, in the morning. Afternoon all right?"

"That'll be fine. I'll come down to the corral right after lunch."

Brenna encountered Stuart's amused eyes when she started upstairs, and she flushed. She wasn't too proud of her actions, but she felt an overwhelming need to be with Brown, and the hours dragged out interminably until it was time to meet him.

He waited for her, the horses already saddled, when she came around the side of the stable. One foot rested on the corral fence, and he stood motionless, gazing northward. She caught her breath as she looked at him—how graceful he was in stillness or in movement!

He turned and saw her, and for a moment his deep-set eyes gleamed.

"Ready?" he said, holding out his hand to help her into the saddle. "Where you want to go?"

"I don't care where we go. Sorry I had to trick you into going with me, but you'd been avoiding me, and I wanted to find out why."

They rode westward for several miles, before he said, "You know why."

"Are you blaming yourself for what happened? It was as much my fault as yours."

"But it can't happen again. Best thing is to stay apart."

Brenna knew he was right, and she had no reply. She

turned her attention to the countryside and saw they were heading toward *Wakantepee*, the high mesa where she'd gone with Dove a few weeks ago.

When they reached the mesa, Brown dismounted and reached out his hand to Brenna. He tethered the horses to a bush and smiled. "Don't want them to run away, like the last time."

He led her to the edge of the mesa. "The ground is dry. Want to sit down?" He sat beside her but kept a safe distance.

"Dove told me this is a sacred place for the Sioux."

"Once was—very little sacred left to us now. Here I came to commune with the Great Spirit. Stayed here for three days, fasting, before my quest was given."

"Can you tell what the Great Spirit revealed to you?"

"Never told anyone, but I'll tell you today—that's why I brought you here. *Wakantanka* said I would be a leader among my people, that in some way I would be able to deliver the Sioux from their troubles. When I awoke from my vision, an eagle feather lay beside me. It was a sign to me that the Great Spirit had spoken."

Brenna wanted to ask questions, but the intensity in his expression discouraged her.

"That's one reason I went away to Carlisle. I thought I would learn the way to lead my people. And what did it do? Turned me into a white man, bred in me a love for the white man's way until I no longer desire to fulfill my quest. The more I love my life of ease at the Bar C, the more I hate myself. The war raging inside me," he struck his chest with his fist, "must be over soon. I cannot stand so much fighting. One must be victorious—the white man or the Sioux."

"And what if the Sioux wins?" Brenna whispered.

"I'll go back to the reservation, try to lead my people, fulfill my vision."

"But what can you do? All I've heard since I've been here is that the Sioux are doomed. What could *you* do?"

"Die with them, mebbe. If I knew some magic way to bring them out of their trouble, I'd try."

Brenna thought of the touchstone. Did she have the magic to prevent Sioux destruction? The necklace troubled her all the time; she had to do something with it. She shook her head—it was wicked to be superstitious about a piece of jewelry.

He moved closer to her and took her hand. She reacted to his touch as she always did—a faint breathlessness invaded her body, and she yearned for his caresses.

"No place for a woman in my life. Cannot let anybody stand between me and my duty to the Great Spirit."

"But what if the white man wins?"

"There is always Kirby and the fact that I am a Sioux and you are not."

She almost told him then of her mysterious past. Would it make any difference?

"Leaving me out of it, what would you *like* to do?"

"Have a ranch of my own, I guess. I saved my money to buy cows. Last year, every male Indian was promised a half section of land." He paused for a long time, looking out across the Bar C holdings; then he put a hand to his breast, and Brenna thought the dismal expression on his face would haunt her the rest of her life. "But I don't think the white man will win."

She started to stand, and he leaped up to help her. "Thanks for telling me, Brown. Whoever wins the battle, I want you to be happy."

"Never be happy, I think." They rode home in silence.

7

*B*y the middle of May the weather settled down, and spring rushed across the Bar C. The pastures sported a fresh green carpet. Each day, migrating birds heading northward dotted the skyline, and many ducks stopped for a few days to forage in the clear snow water that fed the creek. As soon as their day's work was done, cowboys lined the creek banks with fishing poles, and fresh catfish added a great deal to the ranch's daily fare.

In tune with these changes, Brenna's blood stirred to new life, too, as if spring had wrought miraculous transformations in her own body. For the first time in her life, she felt like a *woman*.

Brenna tried to assess her feelings for Kirby, who'd become very attentive. If he asked her to marry him, would she accept? She'd have to look a long time before she found a better mate, and if Brown hadn't entered the picture, she probably wouldn't have hesitated at all. But he had, so she kept holding Kirby off, avoiding having to answer.

In spite of her romantic turmoil, Brenna hadn't lost sight of her real purpose for being in Nebraska. *You're here to write a history of the Sioux nation and to search out your own ancestry,* she reminded herself frequently, and her own personal future had to be set aside until she'd accomplished that. Her conscience often suggested that it wouldn't be right to enter into a marriage with anyone until she unraveled the mystery about her past. Almost daily she looked at the touchstone and wondered what part it had played, or would play, in her life.

Sometimes she thought that everyone at the Bar C had just accepted her as a permanent resident, so at supper one Saturday evening, she said, "Isn't the weather stable enough now for me to do some traveling on the reservation? I've been here almost two months, and while it's been a pleasant visit, I'm eager to start working. Sitting Bull said I could visit his camp, and I want to go before he changes his mind."

"The weather is never stable here," Kirby said with a laugh, "but probably you'd have no trouble." He turned to Dove and Brown. "What do you think? Wonder where the chief is now."

"He's been camping close to Pine Ridge since he left here, but he'll be heading northward soon," Brown said.

Dove darted a furtive look at her brother. "My school is out next week. I'll have a closing program Friday afternoon, and I hope all of you will come. I could go with you, Brenna, after that."

"That will be fine. I'm doing much better with my horseback riding, so I think I can travel well enough."

Frowning, Kirby said, "I don't like to have the two of you traveling around by yourselves, and neither Stuart nor I can leave very well with the spring roundup going on. Why don't you go with them, Brown?"

He surprised Brenna by agreeing readily. "I'll go. Been wanting to spend time with my people." He turned to her. "No easy trip though. Means sleeping on the ground. Sure you want to go?"

"Yes. That's what I came out here to do." With a smile, she added, "I'm not as citified as I look."

For a moment the curtains over his eyes lifted, and she saw naked passion unleashed. "I know," he said. Then his face became expressionless again.

When Brenna went down on Friday morning, ready to leave for Pine Ridge, and Dove's school program, Brown waited for her on the front porch. Raindrop and Brown's favorite horse, Midnight, stood saddled at the hitching rail. Brown tied Brenna's satchel to a mule, already loaded with provisions.

Brenna indicated several cedar poles tied across the top of the load. "What're those for? Firewood?"

"Tepee. Have to have shelter of some kind."

Kirby came from the corrals to see them off, and before he helped Brenna mount, he drew her close and kissed her on the forehead. "Have a good time, but don't forget me."

"I couldn't do that."

Brown swung into his saddle in one fluid movement, and his face gave no hint if he'd seen Kirby's caress. Brown raised his hand in a silent farewell, and Brenna waved to Mendy, who watched from the porch, sniffing into a handkerchief she kept handy for such occasions.

"You watch out for her, Mistah Brown. If I ain't there to watch her, she's liable to get into trouble."

Leading the mule, Brown headed northeast across the pasture, and Brenna followed, marveling at the change in her companion. No hint of civilization remained. Dressed in buckskin breeches and shirt, he wore moccasins, and his hair was tied into two plaits hanging over his shoulders.

When they rode out into the open range, Brown held in his horse until Brenna rode beside him.

"Thanks. I don't like to look at your back all the time," she said, which wasn't exactly the truth, because she'd admired the way his muscles rippled beneath the tight buckskin.

"Indian's woman always rides behind."

She grimaced slightly, pondering once again how he would react if he learned she was part Sioux. "Am I an Indian's woman?"

He threw his arm wide in a questioning gesture. "Who knows? No harm to dream."

His reply startled Brenna, and she thought it might be well that Dove would join them before they traveled much farther. She could never read Brown's mind, and certainly she didn't have much control over her own emotions where he was concerned.

"So you have dreams?"

"That's all the Sioux have left—dreams," he said bitterly. "One thing the white man can't take away from us. Everything else is gone."

"I'm sorry."

"I do not blame you, Brenna. Lots of good white people. I like them. Government men who don't know Sioux—them I hate."

The schoolroom was already crowded when they arrived. Twenty children sat on the front benches, and adults ranged themselves on others around the walls. Brenna and Brown pushed their way into the back of the little log building.

Several smaller children gave short recitations, but the main part of the program consisted of a play, which the students had obviously written themselves. They portrayed Custer's last battle with the Sioux—one of the few victories the Indians could boast of in their conflict with the whites.

Dove's accomplishments with the children surprised and pleased Brenna, and she hurried to compliment her. The rest of the adult audience tramped out without a word when the program concluded.

"That's over," Dove said with a sigh. "Now for a few days of freedom! I'm as bad as the children. When spring comes, I've had enough of the classroom."

"Which way are we going?" Brown asked her. "Where's Sitting Bull now?"

"Two of the Hunkpapa children finished school today, so he's moving camp. I talked with him and told him we wanted to bring Brenna with us for a visit. He remembered her, and it's all right. He's going into the Badlands before he goes back to Standing Rock. So instead of following him, maybe we'd better cut straight to the agency."

"Why's he going to the Badlands?"

Dove looked around guardedly and answered Brown in sign language.

"Safe?"

Dove shrugged her shoulders. "As anywhere. But Brenna shouldn't go."

They talked in Sioux, so Brenna knew they didn't want her to hear, but she caught the general gist of the conversation.

"Won't hurt to take her. She's okay."

Reverting to English, Dove said, "Brenna can sleep in here with me. You eat with us, then bed down somewhere close by, so we'll start early in morning. Sitting Bull's going to leave tonight."

Brenna hoped Dove would explain the strange conversation, but she made no reference to it, so when they started northward the next morning, Brenna speculated more than once what she might encounter before the journey ended.

They caught up with the Indians in mid-afternoon.

"We'll stay behind them, to one side," Brown said. "Sitting Bull will not like it if we go around."

The procession must have been strung out for two or three miles. Women walked beside horses pulling travois loaded with tepee poles and other possessions. Children and dogs raced far and wide, but they kept pace with the adults. Most of the men were mounted, and from a distance the procession looked picturesque, but even as Brenna recorded her impressions of it in a notebook, she remembered her encounter with Indian life at the Bar C and knew how crude and wretched it would appear on close inspection.

In spite of the heat that increased as the day progressed, the large crowd of Indians, which Brenna numbered around two hundred, moved rapidly. In the late afternoon they crossed the White River into a land of stillness and desolation.

Brenna scanned a marching sea of buttes, pinnacles, and haystack hills, through which trickled a kaleidoscope of blues, pinks, greens, and yellows, shifting constantly as evening's gray shadows enveloped the small green valley the Sioux chose for their camp. At first the stillness smothered her—no insect noises, no chirping birds—and she thought the area completely desolate until she saw a prairie dog town on a grassy knoll to their left and noted a few deer sprinting away as the Sioux approached.

In a matter of minutes, the Sioux camp developed as if by magic. Soon thirty tepees were erected, the large one in the center belonging to Sitting Bull. In front of every tepee, a fire burned, and the Indian women started supper.

They moved in then, and after Brown took their greetings to Sitting Bull and received permission to camp with the Hunkpapas, he stretched out on the ground while Dove lifted the heavy poles from the mule's back.

Giving Brown an indignant look, Brenna said, "I'll help, but you'll have to tell me what to do."

First they lashed the tops of three poles together with rawhide strips, to make a tripod, which they anchored to a stake that Dove drove into the ground. They leaned the other poles against the tripod, forming a circular base at the bottom, tied them in place, and finally stretched a wide strip of canvas over the pole framework.

"Most tepees were covered with buffalo hides, but no more are to be had now," Dove explained.

Perhaps sensing Brenna's resentment against her brother, as they worked, Dove said, "Brown is now used to the white man's life, and he would prefer to help me, but Indian ways are rigid. If he did what is considered 'women's work,' everybody'd laugh at him, call him an old woman. He would lose his manhood."

"Fiddle-faddle! He could show his manhood by wrestling these heavy things." Brenna panted.

"You do not need to help. I will finish soon."

Brenna shook her head, gritted her teeth, and kept working.

After finishing the tepee erection, Dove searched for wood and started the fire. "Would you go for water, please, Brenna?" She motioned toward the creek. "It would not be well for you to appear lazy."

Brenna tottered to her feet, grabbed a bucket, and headed toward the stream. *You wanted to find out how the Sioux lived, didn't you? Quit bellyaching.*

Though she had a pail full when she left the creek, she sloshed a third of it on her full riding skirt, leaving only enough water to start their meal. When she started to sit down, Dove said, "Would be a help if you unloaded the rest of things from the mule. I need the dried vegetables Tatoke sent along."

Brenna struggled to untie the tight thongs, stumbling as she carried the heavy bags into the tepee. In spite of her tugging, one knot would not come untied, and she moved to Brown, kicking him, none too gently, on the leg.

He opened his eyes, and she glared at him. "Give me your knife."

"Why?"

"I want to cut that rope."

"Don't cut the rope—we'll need it later." He stirred to his

feet, and with a few deft movements, he freed the knot that had caused her the trouble. Then he stretched out on the ground again.

"Thank you, Your Majesty."

No answer, and she seethed. Dove had said he'd be different out here, but she didn't expect him to be downright lazy. Looking around the camp, though, she noted no other man doing any work.

Dove had the meal prepared in a short time, and the food did a lot to assuage Brenna's temper. She went with Dove to the creek to wash the utensils they'd used, but when Dove announced her intention to visit the women in the camp, Brenna said, "Will it be safe for me to walk to the top of that butte? I'll take my notebook and record the camp activities."

"Brown?" Dove looked at her brother, who rested again. He raised himself up on one elbow and glanced toward the sun, nearing the western horizon amidst a blaze of crimson.

"Won't be dark for a while. Safe enough, but stay in sight of camp."

Still peeved at what she considered Brown's callousness, she started off at a rapid pace and was panting for breath before she reached her destination. She slumped down on the ground. Nothing like a good stiff climb to get rid of anger! But she didn't do much writing, because the Indians weren't doing a great deal to record. The men clustered together in front of Sitting Bull's tepee; the women stood around in another group. Only the children showed much sign of life.

She didn't hear Brown until he squatted beside her and looked at the page of her notebook, still far from filled.

"Finished?"

"There isn't much to write about. Nobody's doing anything. I've written a description of the camp area, which I find interesting and picturesque."

He lifted her to her feet, and holding her hand, he walked around the butte, out of sight of the tepees below.

"I thought you said to stay where you could see them."

"When you're alone. All right with me."

"It's going to be dark soon—shouldn't we go back?"

"I can see." He led her into a rocky hollow between two buttes, where the evening shadows brought a cooling relief from the hot sun they'd endured all day. They sat on a smooth rock, shoulders touching, and leaned back against a rugged spire towering over them.

"I don't like to see Dove do work alone—learned that from the white man. But she understands. Didn't want *you* mad at me."

"I can't see why it would hurt for you to help."

"A good system, Brenna. Man has his work; woman her work. Same way with the white man."

"I don't see any comparison."

"Does a white man cook? Tend a baby? Wash clothes?"

Brenna flushed a little. "I guess not."

"No, he works, makes money, and the woman stays at home. Not so different after all."

"I'm sorry I kicked you. Does it hurt?"

"Felt about like a flea landed on me."

"Oh, you're not as tough as you think you are."

"Not with you." She darted a glance at him and then dropped her gaze. She felt safer when his eyes were expressionless, even though she couldn't read what they said now.

He tipped her head until she had to look at him. "Going to marry Kirby?"

The conversation accelerated too rapidly for Brenna's peace of mind. "He hasn't asked me."

"He will."

"If he does, I'd be a fool to say no, wouldn't I?"

He nodded agreement readily. "True. Kirby's a good man. Make a good husband."

Brenna looked away. "But I don't want him to ask me. There are some complications that would keep me from giving him an answer."

After being silent for several minutes, Brown said finally, "What?"

She breathed deeply and took the plunge. "You, for one."

Strong arms encircled her body and forced her backward on the rock. His face hovered above hers, his eyes burning with intense passion, and when his lips grazed hers, emotion welled through Brenna's body, until she shivered. She wrapped her arms around him and had no idea how long they clung together. Brown stirred first, sat up, and moved away from her.

"A bad complication for you. What are the other problems?"

Brenna had to still her body's reactions before she could answer. Willing her mind to take control and override her rapid pulse, she sat up, lifted a hand to her pulsating throat.

Her voice came out strange and trembly. "What would you say if I told you I'm part Indian?"

He turned startled eyes toward her, taking in every aspect of her facial features. She smiled at his expression.

"Not possible," he said finally.

"I know I don't look it, but I have reason to believe that my mother was Indian, probably Sioux. Do you know that I'm an adopted child?"

He shook his head slowly.

"I am, but that's all I know. The Andersons intended to tell me about my birth when I reached twenty-one. They died a few months before my birthday, but when I went through their things, I found several Sioux items." She told him about the tiny moccasins and the deerskin bag, making no mention of the touchstone. Taking off her jacket, she rolled up the sleeve of her blouse to expose the tatooed circle on her underarm.

He examined it closely. "Sioux marking, all right." He kissed the spot, and goose pimples seared her flesh. Still he looked at her wonderingly. "Sometimes Sioux take captives into tribe. Maybe you're a white baby they had, and they made the mark on you to adopt you into a family."

What he said was highly possible, but there was the touchstone.

"But I want to find out. Will you help? This is the main reason I came out here, thinking I could find some clue to my identity. John Anderson worked at the Red Cloud Agency a long time ago, and when he came back East, he brought me with him."

"A long time ago to find out anything. Thousands of Sioux been killed off in battle or sickness."

"I know I may not find out anything, but will you help me?"

"Yes, but I have to think how to do it." He stood up and pulled her into his arms. "Got to go back to camp."

He kissed her soundly, and said, "If it's true, then *you'll* be a complication to *me*."

8

*T*he next morning Brenna surmised that Dove had something on her mind, for she was unusually quiet. Finally she said, "I think I should tell you why Sitting Bull moved his camp into the Badlands."

"Oh?"

"You know what the sun dance is?"

"Vaguely. I heard Colonel Henry talking to Sitting Bull about it when he visited the Bar C."

"That's the reason for this journey, and I don't think we should stay."

"I thought the government agents had forbidden these sun dances."

"They have, so that's the reason for secrecy." Dove stomped around the tepee, displaying more anger than Brenna had ever known her to show. "This is the Sioux religion, as important as Easter and Christmas to Christians. The government has no right to ban them."

Brenna began to see the significance of the conversation Dove and Brown had before they left Pine Ridge Agency.

"You apparently knew about this before we came. Why this sudden notion to leave?"

"It's *you* I don't think should be here."

"Why not? You don't think I'd report it to the authorities, do you?"

"No," she said after a slight hesitation, "but you might write something in your book. I wouldn't want Sitting Bull to get into trouble because of us. But that's not the main reason; I know something now I didn't know when we left Pine Ridge."

Brown joined them, having just had a bath in the creek. His brown torso glistened with tiny beads of water, and his black hair lay wet against his head. Brenna's blood stirred, and she looked away.

"I don't think Brenna should stay here," Dove said.

"Take her back to the Bar C then."

"But I want to learn about the Sioux," Brenna protested. "Why shouldn't I see this sun dance?"

"You won't like it," Dove warned.

A suspicion formed in Brenna's mind, and she said to Brown, "After you'd been avoiding me for days, why did you agree to come up here with me?"

"Planned to come anyway. Had already made up my mind."

"Made up your mind to do what?"

"Perform the sun dance. Sacrifice my body to the Great Spirit."

So this was why Dove thought she should leave! Brenna's knees knuckled under her, and she sat down suddenly, not trusting her legs to support her.

"Oh, please don't," she whispered, knowing now what he meant to do. She looked over his beautiful physique, scarless now, but what would it look like after he'd endured the sun-dance ritual? She remembered the scars on Sitting Bull's body and shuddered.

He sat beside her and compassionately patted her hand. "You see my body, and you like it this way, but to the other Sioux, I appear weak, less of a man. Twenty-five summers I've lived and not yet made my peace with the Great Spirit. Maybe I'm not a man, maybe can't endure the pain, but I must know, dear one. I must know."

"But, Brown, Christ was the sacrifice for our sins. He died on the cross, gave His life. If you want peace, accept Him as Lord and Savior. Don't go through this ritual; it's wicked. Haven't you heard Christ's plan of salvation? Don't you know that Jesus said, 'I am the way, the truth, and the life: no man cometh unto the Father, but by me'?"

"When I was at Carlisle, I heard of Christ. I was baptized, and there it seemed right to go to the white man's church. But I've not been at peace since I returned home. I am going through the sun dance."

His face wore the same look she'd observed when he had ridden the wild horse, so she buried her face in his shoulder, knowing it was useless to persuade him further.

"Let Dove take you back to Bar C," he insisted.

"Oh, no," she denied quickly. "I won't leave you. If you think you must do this, I'll be there. Whatever you suffer, I'll endure it with you."

"Put on one of Dove's robes then, so you will not look out of place."

She leaned against him, content to feel his strong arms supporting her. "Tell me a little of what's going to happen."

"This morning the medicine man went out to find a cot-tonwood tree. When he finds the right tree, the whole village goes out to cut it down and bring it back to the council circle."

By afternoon the medicine man returned, looking myste-rious, and Brenna assumed the tree had been selected. The next morning she followed the other women to the edge of the forest. A festival spirit prevailed as the women sang, picked flowers as they walked along, and cheered when they came to the tree, which looked like any other tree to Brenna.

At first, a pregnant woman danced around the tree.

"*Wakantanka* loves fruitfulness in women," Dove explained.

A young man went forward and struck the tree, which symbolized the enemy; then he distributed gifts to those near him. Some children ran to hit the sacred tree, and their parents gave presents away.

"Now, it's our turn," Dove said, and she handed Brenna an ax. Brenna followed her to the tree and awkwardly helped several young women trim off the tree's lower branches.

A Sioux brave cut down the tree, and very carefully, small poles were inserted under it, for no one was supposed to touch the trunk. About twenty young men lifted the poles and started toward the village. With her arms full of branches, Brenna trailed the men, who stopped four times before they arrived at the camp.

The first three times they stopped, the medicine man howled like a wolf. After the fourth stop, Brown and several other mounted men raced toward the village.

"God, show me," Brenna prayed. "Should a Christian be involved in such an incident?"

"The first one to touch the holy spot where the tree will stand is safe—will not be killed in battle this year," Dove said.

"I hope Brown is the first one."

He met them when they reached the tepees, and Brenna quickly asked, "Did you touch it first?"

"No, but no matter. Whatever the Great Spirit has for me will be revealed in the sun dance. Come, dear one, help Dove prepare for the feast."

The odor of boiling meat permeated the whole area, for the Indian hunters had been successful in finding a buffalo. Around the smaller fires, women cooked wild turnips and onions. Dove and Brenna made several pans of corn bread. The food would be served communal style, so they wanted enough bread to share.

Brenna looked around for Brown when she awakened the next morning, and Dove explained his absence, "He has gone to the sweat lodge to prepare himself. He and others will not take part in the feasting today. We will not see them."

The council circle had taken on a festive air. The pole stood tall and erect, and a bundle of branches hung on a projecting limb that had been spared for that purpose. Brenna shuddered, for the bundle made the pole look like a cross.

From the crosspiece, black effigies of a buffalo and a man were suspended, as well as buckskin bags filled with tobacco. Underneath the pole, bags of tobacco tied on sticks had been placed as prayer offerings. West of the pole lay a buffalo skull against which a peace pipe leaned, the stem pointing east.

Soon the dancing started, with only young men participating—a shuffling, mournful action, Brenna considered it. Sitting Bull appeared and danced, facing the young men. Some of the dancers took their rifles and shot at the effigies of the buffalo and man.

The sound of the drums frustrated Brenna, but Dove looked entranced. "Oh, how I wish the white man had never come here. I've heard my mother tell about the beauty of sun dances when she was a girl. Hundreds of our people would be present. It was a festive time, a time of renewal." Bitterness entered her voice. "Now we have to sneak around to perform rites that are so important to us."

"But how long has this been going on? What does it mean?"

"Tonight you will learn. Sitting Bull will recite the history of our people. I will interpret for you."

"He told me some things when I saw him at the Bar C, but I don't know how the sun dance figures into it."

Later, when she sat in the council circle, listening to the chant of the medicine men, Brenna felt a stirring in her blood, and for the first time the ceremony took on some significance. In an earlier time, had *her* ancestors sat in such a circle? Had they, too, gone through the ritual of the sun dance?

Sitting Bull hunched before them, surrounded by five medicine men. They passed the sacred pipe from one to the other. The chief's voice rolled across the valley, and Dove whispered his words to Brenna.

"Long ago the Great Spirit sent us the White Buffalo Calf Maiden." He related the story of the buffalo calf that turned into a maiden as he'd told Brenna before.

"She told us how to purify the soul to return it to the Great Spirit," he continued. "Then she taught us the sacred ritual of the sweat lodge."

The chief paused several minutes, and Dove whispered, "The sweat lodge is to make people pure, give them strength for some great undertaking. Brown and the others will leave behind in the lodge all that is impure. When they come out, they will be able to live as *Wakantanka* wishes. I've heard the old men say the experience makes you feel as if you've been born again."

"Oh, no, Dove," Brenna protested, "only Christ is able to cleanse and give a new birth."

She hushed as Sitting Bull spoke. "Tonight we will beseech the Great Spirit that he will send a vision to one of us—a vision that will guide the Sioux nation to be strong and fruitful."

Before she went to sleep, Brenna petitioned God: "Lord, reveal their folly to these people. Is there some way for me to teach them the right way? How can I ease Brown's unhappiness?"

Brenna slept fitfully that night, thinking about Brown in the sweat lodge, contemplating what would happen to him tomorrow. Though she dreaded the day, she longed for daylight, wanting nothing now but to get the sun dance behind them, so they could return to the Bar C.

The ceremony started just before sunrise, so they hurried through breakfast, wanting to be at the sacred circle when Brown came.

Drummers pounded buffalo skins, and several men came from the sweat lodge. A leader carried the peace pipe, with the others following one by one. All of them wore buffalo robes. Brenna tried to catch Brown's gaze, but she might have been a stranger, for all the notice he gave her. His eyes held a faraway look, and she believed he'd forgotten her existence.

When they neared the pole, the dancers shed the buffalo robes and put on headdresses ornamented with porcupine-quill work, which matched the similarly decorated pieces of buckskin that dangled from their waists like skirts. The leader gave each of them an eagle-bone whistle to put in their mouths.

Brenna's mind was so muddled that she didn't know if she was praying to *Wakantanka* or to her own God, but she whispered, "I don't know what he wants, but fulfill his wishes. Let him prove that he's all man, that he's still a Sioux."

Four other men waited with Brown, and after the medicine men painted their bodies, the five participants lay down on the ground as though they were dead. With a quick movement, a medicine man made two slashes on Brown's chest with a knife. Brenna groaned as she saw blood running down his chest, but she tried to compose herself when Dove shook her head, and muttered, "If you can't take it, leave. Don't dare interfere."

The medicine man pulled down a strip of rawhide that hung from the crosspiece, and pushed the leather through the slashes on Brown's chest, and tied it in place. Brenna knew that he must be suffering agony, but no trace of pain crossed his face. She was proud of him. No one could doubt he was all Sioux, if only he could endure the long hours of suffering.

When the four other men received similar gashings, all of them stood up to dance back and forth, leaning on the rawhide strip, facing the rising sun. The drumbeats rolled back and forth through the little valley, and each time the drum was struck, the dancers blew the whistles in their mouths.

The dancing figures blurred before Brenna's eyes, and Dove grabbed her arm to drag her away from the sacred circle. When Brenna came to herself, she lay on her back in the tepee, and Dove sat beside her.

"What time is it?" she said through parched lips. "Are they still dancing?"

"Near noon."

Dove didn't answer the other question, but hearing the sounds of the drumbeats and the chanting, Brenna knew the answer. She sat up.

"I have to go back. Are you coming?"

Dove nodded, and they made their way toward the council circle. Two of the dancers had already crumpled and lay unconscious on the ground, but Brown and the others still danced, tugging at the rawhide strips, staring toward the sun.

"He must be ready to collapse," Brenna whispered to Dove. "He hasn't had anything to eat all day."

"He won't drop until his skin breaks, and that could be hours yet."

So weak herself that she could hardly stand, Brenna sat on the ground, leaning against a rock, and agonized for Brown. Remembering the torture he'd taken when he'd ridden the wild horse at the Bar C, she knew that he had strong powers of endurance and didn't doubt that he'd go through this whole torturous ritual without a sound.

The sun went down, and still he danced. Around midnight, the rawhide mercifully severed his skin, and Brown tumbled to the ground. Brenna started to him, but Dove held her back.

"You must not. Now is the time for his vision, if *Wakantanka* sends one. He may lie there all night. Come, let us return to the tepee."

Brenna knew Dove was right. She longed to wash his body and bring him a drink of water, but she was an outsider here. She wouldn't shame Brown by doing anything to comfort his body.

"You go to the tepee, if you want to, but I'm going to stay. If he comes to and wants something, I'll be here."

Dove walked away without answering, but soon she returned with two blankets. "The night is cold," she said as she handed one blanket to Brenna and wrapped up in the other one.

Day dawned before Brown regained consciousness. He sat up slowly, and the medicine men gathered around him.

Faintly, he said, "The Great Spirit say to me that the White Buffalo Calf Maiden will soon appear to us. It'll be my privilege to recognize her. I do not know how, but the Spirit says that when I see her, the sign will be plain."

"That is good," one of the medicine men said. "The maiden promised to look in upon us in every age. In my time, I have not seen her. We will welcome the return of the maiden."

Brenna wasn't interested in the Buffalo Calf Maiden, but she did want to help Brown, who wove unsteadily on his feet when he tried to stand. She stifled a sob and tried to be patient until he started wobbling toward them, and she waited no longer.

"Oh, Brown, let me help you to the tepee."

He smiled and leaned against her when she placed an arm around him. With Dove on the other side, they walked slowly to the tepee and eased him down on a blanket.

"Does it hurt much?" Brenna whispered.

"Great Spirit took away the hurt."

"If you'll cleanse the wound, I'll prepare some food," Dove said as she bustled out of the tepee.

A container of water stood outside the tepee, and Brenna poured some of it in a pan. She pulled a cloth from her bag and wiped his face carefully. His eyes followed her every movement as she washed his body.

"You are good to wait on me."

She laid her fingers on his lips. "You should rest."

"Your hands on my body do not bring rest—only a hunger that can never be fed."

She leaned over him, trying to spare his sore body, and pressed her lips against his. He surprised her by drawing her down to him, for she'd thought his strength was spent.

Dove's step drew them apart. If she'd seen the embrace, she didn't mention it. "I have ointment for his wound. Do you want to apply it?" She backed out of the tepee without another word.

As Brenna carefully rubbed the salve into his wound, she asked, "Are you happy now that you have proven your manhood?"

"Happiness I do not know. I have lived up to the tradition of my fathers, and that is good."

"No one can doubt your courage. I think you stood the pain better than I did, for I cringed at your agony. I've decided I must not be Sioux after all."

"I have a mission from the Great Spirit. He said to me that I should return to my people."

"You mean leave the Bar C?" she gasped.

He nodded, and she threw her arms around him, easing up when he flinched. "And I've been counting the minutes until we could go back. There's no future for you here. You know the Sioux nation is about finished. Please don't do anything so foolish, Brown."

He pushed her hands away. "What the Great Spirit has spoken, I will do."

She knew then that she'd lost him, if you can lose something you've never had. He now did the bidding of *Wakantanka*, and she no longer mattered to him. The battle was over—the Indian had won.

9

*B*rown slept on the mat all day. Dove and Brenna moved quietly, to avoid wakening him, and no noise infiltrated from the rest of the camp to disturb his slumber. Now that the sun dance had ended, most of the Indians dozed in the sun. Though she'd spent a sleepless night, Brenna had never felt less like resting. She fidgeted around the tepee until Dove finally said, "Why not take a walk? Brown needs rest, and you're going to awaken him if you don't quiet down."

Without a word, Brenna left the tepee. Already the sun's rays drenched the arid land, and a strong breeze swept across the valley, whipping her skirts around her legs. To harness her thoughts, Brenna concentrated on the high peaks, sharp ridges, and buttes around her. Her imagination turned the natural phenomena into castles and statues. But for all its beauty, the place seemed dead to her, and she considered it a fitting camp for this dying people.

How much longer would the Sioux survive as a nation? And what about Brown? With his education and the help Kirby would give him, he could go a long way. He could easily become a rancher, but if he returned to the Sioux, he'd soon be living in squalor like these other Indians.

Why should it matter to you? she chided. Could she admit that she loved this man? Was that what sparked the tumult throughout her body when he touched her? If she loved Brown, how could she define the warm, comfortable feeling she harbored for Kirby?

Not for the first time, Brenna wished she'd never left Philadelphia, but she would still try to save Brown from himself. After all, his vision probably wasn't anything more than hallucinations. He hadn't eaten for hours, and he'd undergone intense suffering—no wonder he'd passed out. Vision indeed!

Brown roused soon after she returned to the tepee. Dove had prepared food, and she handed a bowl of stew to her brother. Brenna dipped out a helping for herself.

"Sitting Bull intends to move the camp to Standing Rock tomorrow. What are we going to do?" Dove said.

"I'll take you back to Bar C."

"And you?" Dove asked.

"I not know now." He flashed a glance in Brenna's direction. "I have complications, too," he said with a slight smile.

Later in the evening, Brown took Brenna's hand. "Walk?" he said.

He led her to the little alcove they'd visited three nights before, where the silence overwhelmed her. Sitting on the same rock, Brown reached for her, but Brenna shoved his hands away.

"No, Brown. I want to talk to you about something, and when you kiss me, I get all mixed up."

He leaned back against the rock, resting his hand on her shoulder. He drew his forefinger down across her face, and Brenna squirmed at the touch. She moved away until his hand slid from her shoulder.

"Did you mean what you said about going to live on the reservation?"

He nodded.

"Please don't do that without giving it a lot of thought. I know you're concerned about your people, and I hate to see the way they've been treated myself. But what can you do? You're only one person, after all, and you've lived so many years away from the Sioux. I think you'd be miserable."

"When I roused from the vision, I was sure. The sign had been given. But now I doubt. *You* are the complication. Even if you marry Kirby, if I live at Bar C, I can see you, feast on your beauty. On the reservation, I'll not see you at all. I don't like that."

"I don't like that either, but there's no reason you can't help the Sioux by living as the whites do. In fact, you might be even more help to them that way. You're smart, you've got so much to give, and it would just be wasted if you live like this." She swung her arm to indicate the Sioux camp. "Look at Sitting Bull—once a great leader, now harried from one reservation to another."

She didn't like the expression on his face, but she hurried on. "I inherited a lot of money when my parents died— enough to provide you with a ranch of your own. I could help you in lots of other ways, too."

"If you marry Kirby, he might not like it."

"You're taking a lot for granted. I told you he hasn't asked me, and I don't know that I'd say yes if he did."

"I don't understand what you want to tell me. Speak plain."

She took a deep breath. "I mean, if you come to the reservation to live, that ends everything for us. If you were a rancher, it might be different."

His expression was incredulous. "If I used your money to start a ranch, you'd marry me."

Brenna felt her face coloring. Was she really suggesting such a thing? Practically asking this man to marry her?

"Maybe."

Eyes alight with passion, Brown leaned over her again. This time she didn't push him away, but before his lips claimed hers and she lost all power to reason, she said hurriedly, "But not if you come to the reservation."

After what seemed like hours of unbearable ecstasy, Brenna freed her lips. "Oh, Brown, please don't kiss me like that again."

"Great love I feel for you, Brenna. Precious to me—I wouldn't want to see you live in a tepee. You belong in a big house like at Bar C."

She sat up and clutched his arm. "Then let's build one together," she said breathlessly. "We could be happy, I know we could."

He pulled her into his arms again. Not passionately this time, but with a soft caress. "I'll go back to the Bar C with you but I cannot forget my vision. The Great Spirit told me that I would have a further sign about the Buffalo Calf Maiden. I will await the sign."

On the way back to the ranch, Brenna had no chance to talk with Brown alone, and perhaps that was just as well. She felt guilty trying to persuade him to forsake what he considered a mission from the Great Spirit. Sometimes she felt like a harlot—almost as if she'd offered her body to persuade him to her ways.

They stopped for the night at Dove's schoolroom and to gather the things she'd need for the summer. While they were there, one of the women brought Brenna's buckskin dress that Dove had ordered for her. Too tired to try on the garment, she held it up to her body and decided it would be a good fit.

Arriving at the Bar C, Brenna noted with relief that Kirby

was away. She needed some time away from Brown to compose herself. But when Kirby came into the house with Stuart at his heels, she realized her feelings for him hadn't changed at all.

He kissed her lightly on the lips. "Welcome home, Brenna. We've missed you."

"Sure have," Stuart agreed. "Know any more about the Sioux now than you did before you left?"

"Lots more, and some of it I'd be just as well off not to know."

"I figured that," he said.

"Has anyone told you?" Kirby asked.

"Told me what?"

"Mendy has run away."

Brenna stared at him. "Run away!" she shrieked.

"To get married."

"Married! At her age. Who's the lucky guy, may I ask?' Then remembering, she added, "To that cowhand of yours, I suppose."

Kirby laughed. "That's right. They left two days ago. She told Tatoke they were going on a honeymoon but that they'd be back in a few weeks. She left a note for you."

"She's free to do what she wants to, but to think that she insisted on coming out here to chaperone *me*."

"We'll have to kill the fatted calf when they return," Kirby said. "I have a house they can live in."

Although she'd had no reason to ever suspect Mendy's honesty, Brenna hurried upstairs and searched her luggage. Some of her money had been taken. In its place was a note: "Miss Brenna. I tuk a few coins, for I didn't have much money with me. You can take it from what Mistah John left me when we get back home. We'll be back in a few days. I'm in love."

Well, love does strange things, Brenna had to admit. *Look at the mess I'm in.*

A few nights later, in a reckless mood, Brenna dressed in the white buckskin garment, and as a final touch, she draped the touchstone around her neck. Feeling like some tribal princess who could wield power over everyone she saw, she brushed her hair over her shoulders and put a white band around her forehead.

Glancing in the mirror, she admired again the beauty of the necklace. Her white dress heightened the intensity of the black jade and the gold streaks shone like random rays of sunshine on a rainy day.

Stuart always came to supper on Sunday, and she waited until she heard him and Brown join Kirby in the parlor. She walked softly down the steps and entered the room with a flourish.

"*Hou, cola!* I'm White Star, Sioux maiden."

She had expected them to be impressed by her appearance, and Kirby was. He whistled appreciatively. "Pretty nifty outfit you've got there."

Brown and Stuart weren't impressed. Shock seemed a better way to describe their reaction, and they stared at her, stupefied.

Brown found his voice first, and he whispered, "*Piedra de toque. Piedra de toque.* My sign from the Great Spirit. You're the White Buffalo Calf Maiden."

"So that's where it went!" Stuart shouted.

Brenna covered the gleaming stone with her hand. At that moment Dove entered the room, and said to Brenna, "You look like a real Indian girl now."

Brown walked to Brenna and took her hand away from the touchstone. He pointed at it, and Dove's face paled. "Is it what I think?" she asked.

Her brother nodded and turned piercing eyes on Brenna. "Where'd you get it?"

Brenna backed away from him.

"Will someone tell me what's going on?" Kirby demanded. "What's so important about that necklace?"

"I think we'd better sit down," Stuart said.

"It's time to eat," Kirby insisted.

Nobody ate much. To Brenna, the touchstone felt as if it might burn a hole right between her breasts, and when Tatoke, sighting the stone, dropped a plate of bread right in the middle of the dining room floor, Brenna hid the necklace inside her dress.

Back in the living room, Stuart took charge, and looking at Brenna, he said kindly, "Can you tell us where you got the necklace and how long you've had it?"

She pulled the touchstone from the front of her dress, saying, "I'd not seen this until a few months ago. When I opened Dad's trunk after his death, I found the touchstone. I don't know how he happened to have it."

"But what's so important about that necklace? Why do you all act as if you've been hoodooed?" Kirby demanded.

"That necklace happens to be the lost *piedra de toque* of the Sioux, or more particularly of Big Foot's band. Some of the Indians are superstitious about that stone and blame a lot of their bad fortune on its disappearance. It's been gone for several years," Stuart said.

"There were some other things in that trunk. I have them upstairs."

"Let's see them, please," Stuart said.

Brown stood at his favorite place by the fireplace, not even looking at her now. As she walked upstairs, Brenna's legs shook so badly she could barely navigate. She felt sure that the enigma of her birth would soon be no longer a mystery, and now that the time had come, she fervently wished she'd never started on this quest. If only she could run out the front door, hurry to Crawford, and take a train east as fast as she could go! But instead she lifted the trunk lid and took the items down to Stuart.

She wondered at the strange look on Stuart's face when he looked at the baby moccasins and the note, "For my dotter."

"The note was wrapped around the touchstone."

Stuart held the moccasins in his hand, and his eyes were compassionate as he looked at Brenna. "Sit down, my dear. I have something to tell you that I'd never thought you'd need to know. Strange how the things we plan for good often turn out the other way."

"Well, say on," Kirby said impatiently. Brenna had never seen him so edgy before. Was he apprehensive about what all of this drama might reveal?

"I don't know any easy way to tell you that you're *my* daughter, born to me and my Indian wife, Santee. When she left the reservation to live with me, I thought she'd become Americanized, but every so often, she'd go back to the reservation and stay for weeks. When you were born, I forbade her to take you. I loved you, and I was determined that you'd be raised in the white culture."

Now that the information she dreaded had been revealed, Brenna felt only a sense of relief. Stuart was a man any woman would be proud to own as her father.

"How come I never knew you had a daughter?" Kirby demanded.

"Not very many people did. I didn't come to the Bar C until after that. One day, when I discovered that Santee had tatooed your arm with a Sioux symbol, I knew she'd never be happy until you were all Sioux. I took you to John Anderson and asked him to take you and raise you as his own."

Brenna pulled up her sleeve and revealed the circle on her arm. "It's still there."

Stuart nodded. "If I needed any proof, that would be it. I gave John Anderson the gold I'd found to pay for your keep."

"Which he never used at all. The account hadn't been touched when he died. It's mine now."

"I didn't want to give you up, but I didn't try to keep in contact with you. I did what I thought was best for you. Three years ago, when White Dove came home from a visit to the Andersons was the first time I'd heard anything about you."

As far as Stuart and Brenna were concerned, they might have been the only two people in the room. Was this the reason she'd been drawn to Stuart right from the first? Would it be so difficult to accept the fact that she had mixed blood, since he was her real father?

"But what about these things?" Brenna asked, touching the necklace and pointing to the leather bag. "How did Dad get them?"

"I have no idea, unless Santee slipped them to John without my knowledge. I guess we'll never know."

"But why should she send away an item like the touchstone?"

"Maybe she thought that was the one way to keep you safe and bring you back to the Sioux. The stone has been lost before, but it's always found its way back to the tribe."

Brenna took the chain from around her neck. "To whom should I give this? I certainly don't want to keep anything the Sioux value." She handed the touchstone to Dove. "Here. Maybe you can find out what to do with it."

Brown moved quickly toward her. "No, you take it. You're the White Buffalo Calf Maiden. The Great Spirit showed me the sign. Go to the reservation with me. Save the Sioux."

"Hold on a minute," Kirby bellowed. "Go to the reservation with you! And what's all this about the buffalo maiden? It's not like you to speak so foolishly, Brown."

Brown turned toward Kirby, his eyes blazing. "I had a vision. The White Buffalo Calf Maiden is coming again. I was to receive a sign. The *piedra de toque*, it is the sign."

Kirby turned toward Brenna. "You don't believe anything like that, do you?"

Turning troubled brown eyes toward him, Brenna said, "I don't know what to think. I'm so mixed up." She started crying, and Stuart's loud voice silenced them all.

"Now, listen here. Brenna's had about all she can take in one evening. Leave her alone. You go on to bed, Brenna, and when we've all had time to think, we can talk this out."

She stopped sobbing and gulped. "Have you known all along that I was your daughter?"

"Yes, but I didn't think I'd ever have to tell you. It seemed better that you never knew."

"But that's one reason I came west. I wanted to find out who I was."

"Now that you know, are you any better off?"

She wearily shook her head. "No, I guess not. I'm so confused. What should I do?"

"Go to bed now. We can talk about it tomorrow."

Brown reached out a hand to the touchstone that Brenna still held. He lovingly caressed it, much as he had caressed her.

"*Piedra de toque*," he whispered. "You will bring power and prosperity to my people once again."

As she closed the door into her room Brenna realized the wisdom of Stuart's advice about resting, but she also knew that tomorrow wouldn't bring an end to the turmoil she felt.

In spite of the high regard she had for Stuart, anger rose in her at the thought of what he had done. How dare he manipulate her life? If he'd not given her to John Anderson, none of these problems would have arisen.

The tears she'd tried to stifle downstairs began to flow freely, cleansing her of bitterness and anger. But crying brought a stuffed-up head and smarting eyes, and did nothing to help with the decision she'd faced for days. What was she going to do about Brown?

10

Stuart waited in the parlor when Brenna came down-stairs the next morning. No one else was around, and she guessed the Bar-C residents had planned it that way. She'd felt close to this man right from the first, but now she felt embarrassed in his presence.

"So you're my father. Seems strange, for I just assumed that my parents were both dead."

"I hope you don't blame me for giving you away. I wanted the best for you, and I thought John Anderson could provide it."

A look of pain crossed his face. "You'll never know what it cost me to give you up, but I knew if anything happened to me, Santee would take you back to the reservation."

"How did my mother like having her baby taken away? Did you have any other children?"

"No more children. I hadn't intended to have any at all. But as for taking you away, she protested, of course, but she'd seen Kirby's mother a few times, and she admired her. Maybe she wanted her daughter to be like that."

"Where's she buried? I'd like to see her grave."

Stuart shook his head. "I'm sorry. I took her back to the Sioux, and they gave her a native burial. Her cousin is Big Foot, one of the local chiefs. She was a Miniconjou, the same group Tatoke claims for her family."

"Wonder why I don't look more like the Indians? And whom *do* I look like? I don't look like you."

"You look like my mother. Even if I hadn't known that you were John Anderson's adopted daughter, and so had to be my own offspring, I'd have recognized your resemblance to Mom. And I want you to know, Brenna, that I'm proud of you. You're a credit to me."

"But what should I call you now?"

"Why don't we just go on as we have been for a while? Let's have some breakfast now."

While they ate the biscuits and gravy Tatoke brought, Brenna broached the subject that had kept her awake most of the night. "What do you think of Brown's reaction to all of this? About the White Buffalo Calf Maiden, I mean."

"From what he said, I'm assuming that he went through the sun dance and received some sort of vision."

At Brenna's nod, Stuart continued, "Of course, I don't believe any of that stuff, but it won't be easy to convince Brown that you aren't the answer to his vision."

"What about the touchstone? I don't want to keep the necklace if it belonged to the Indians. Where did they get it?"

Stuart threw wide his arms in a wondering gesture. "Who knows? The story is that the Great Spirit sent it to them and that they've had it always. My guess is that some European explorer lost it out here."

"But *piedra de toque* is a Spanish term, and I'm sure the Spanish didn't explore this far north."

"The Indians ranged great distances as they followed the buffalo, and the way they trade items, it could have changed hands many times. I'd seen it once when I first came to this country. I don't know how long Santee had it, but she had the last laugh on me, I guess. I tried to free you from your Indian culture, and she sent this along with you."

Tatoke entered the room.

"Sit down, Tatoke, and tell us what you know about the touchstone," Stuart invited.

She perched uncomfortably on the edge of a chair. "I don't know where it came from in first place, unless the Great Spirit dropped it down from heaven. Supposed to be, first Sioux to get it stole from his enemy—struck a coup by taking *piedra de toque*. Has changed from tribe to tribe, sometimes by warfare, sometimes trade, sometimes by stealing. He who has it tries to keep it secret from others, so as not to be taken, but a tribe has it, and everyone always knows it's there, because good fortune comes to that tribe."

"Could Santee have stolen the necklace and sent it along when John Anderson took Brenna?"

"Mebbe. Last time I knew where the *piedra de toque* is, it belonged to my uncle, Blue Feather. He had it when I went to live with my man near Fort Laramie. He still had it when I came back. Brown was a little boy then, but he remembers seeing it. Then it disappeared. No one knew where it went. Could be Santee took it."

"Let's figure a little. How old is Brown?"

Tatoke indicated twenty-five with her fingers.

"Then he would have been four years old when you were born, Brenna, so I suppose he could remember it, especially if you've talked to him about it, Tatoke."

"Lots of talk when seemed sure it disappeared. Too bad times for Miniconjou—we thought an enemy had it. Maybe a white man had it, when things go good for them, bad for Sioux. That all I know."

"Thanks, Tatoke. Now we have to decide what to do with it."

"Must go back to our tribe. Our last chance to survive, mebbe."

She picked up some of their breakfast dishes and entered the kitchen.

"At times I've thought the stone might have some mystical power, but it's just a pretty and valuable ornament." Remembering the wretched conditions of Sitting Bull's followers, she commented, "The Sioux would gain a lot more if they'll sell the touchstone and use the money to improve their lives."

"Perhaps," Stuart said, "but they wouldn't see it that way."

"Guess I didn't inherit any Sioux characteristics. I don't look like an Indian; I apparently don't think like one."

"For one thing, you're only a quarter blood. Santee's father wasn't Sioux—he was a French Canadian trapper who lived with the tribe."

"I wonder if Kirby's opinion of me will change, now that he knows I'm part Sioux."

"Why not let Kirby answer that?" Kirby said as he came into the room. "You've had her to yourself long enough, Stuart. Now it's my turn."

Tatoke entered the room with a cup of steaming coffee and set it in front of Kirby, who'd dropped into the chair beside Brenna.

"Absence makes the heart grow fonder, and you've been gone several days. As for your being part Indian, that doesn't matter. After all, my father married a Sioux, and that worked out all right. So I'm asking you now, before you go away from me again: Will you marry me? I've tried to ask before, but you avoided the question."

Brenna wilted in her seat. "Oh, Kirby, I don't know. I wouldn't let you ask me before because of the secret surrounding my past. Now that's cleared up, but I still can't give you an answer."

"Take your time—how about letting me know tomorrow?" he said smilingly.

"But I didn't come out here to be married."

"Why *did* you come?"

"To find out who I am and to research and finish Dad's book."

"The first is solved. You can write that book better here at the Bar C than in Philadelphia." He seemed to have forgotten that Stuart remained in the room. "Please say yes, Brenna. I love you, and I'm lonely. I didn't know how lonely until you came along."

Memories of Brown's caresses clouded her mind. "I don't know that I love you, Kirby. I admire you greatly, but I haven't sorted out my feelings."

"You've been my dream girl for three years now, and I love the real girl even more than the dream. Stuart, you talk to her, tell her what a great husband I'd be." He spoke this last sentence jokingly, but Brenna detected the depth of his emotion by the gravity of his eyes.

Then Kirby suddenly laughed aloud. "If she takes me up on that offer, you'll be my father-in-law."

"Well, so what?" Stuart answered banteringly. "That should be an added bonus."

Kirby stood, obviously still amused at the thought. "I don't know about that. I have to hurry—I'm supposed to be in Crawford by ten o'clock. See you tonight."

Making preparations to leave himself, Stuart commented, "He would make a good husband, you know."

Brenna stared stormily at Stuart. "I'm getting tired of being told something I already know. That isn't what's bothering me."

"Sure, I know that. You're my daughter, remember?"

"Then tell me what to do about Brown."

"That, I can't do. If you go with Brown, it'll be a mistake, but everyone has the right to make some mistakes in a lifetime. Think carefully before you do anything."

"The smart thing for me to do is pack up today and head back to Philadelphia. Don't you agree?"

"Go ahead, but you'll come back. The call to adventure is in your blood—you can't blot that out."

Brenna even went so far as to pack her trunk, but she knew she couldn't take the coward's way out.

Once that morning Dove came and knocked softly on the door, but Brenna didn't answer. Nor did she go downstairs to lunch. But she couldn't put off the inevitable, and in early afternoon, when she saw Brown coming toward the house, leading her horse, she went downstairs. She met him at the door.

"Want to go for ride?" His hopeful smile shattered her slight defenses.

"No. I realize we have to talk, but I'll feel safer here in the parlor. When we're alone, you take advantage of my weakness. I can't always think the way I should."

"Okay." He motioned her toward the big room.

Brown stood by the mantel, and Brenna sat down near him. He said nothing, but he looked at her as though she were a ripe apple ready to be plucked, and it disconcerted her.

"I *am not* the White Buffalo Calf Maiden."

"Mebbe not."

"I will give you the touchstone. You take it where you think it should go."

He shook his head slowly.

"Now, Brown, don't be stubborn."

"You're the sign promised by Great Spirit. I would not ask you otherwise. I know life is hard there, but I must do what is necessary to help my people. If you live among us, you'll give us new spirit, new life."

Remembering the indolence of Sitting Bull's followers,

Brenna realized they needed a new spirit, but it wouldn't come from her or the touchstone. Besides, it would be impossible for her to live as the Sioux did.

"I would never have asked you to marry me before. I'm not good enough for you—too different. But now I have the sign. If you come to the reservation as my wife—well and good. If not, come to live among us anyway. Dove and my mother would come too, so you would not be lonely."

As she listened to him, Brenna thought ironically that the touchstone hadn't brought her peace and plenty. Plenty maybe, if she considered the large amount of money she'd inherited, but the thing had caused her more turmoil in six months than she'd known in all of the twenty years before that.

Mentally, she could have pushed to one side any thought of becoming a Sioux woman, but she had to admit, when she looked at Brown, that physically she wasn't her own master. Considering marriage to this man caused her blood to churn like the raging ocean beat along the shore. Without Brown, she'd never be content again, but was stilling that storm worth the sacrifice it required?

"I will go with you to the reservation as your wife." Even as she had said the words, Brenna wondered if it was actually she who had spoken. Without even a thought of Kirby, she'd given her answer.

Brown reached her in one big leap and gathered her into his arms in an embrace that made her gasp for breath.

"My love!" he murmured. "My heart burns for your spirit. My body burns for your favors. I feel deepness of love in my soul."

Tears smarted her eyes, and Brenna felt moisture on her face as her arms crept around his neck. "And I love you," she said. "I don't care anything about the rest of the Sioux, but I do want to make you happy."

Clinging lips sealed their pledges. Then Brenna pulled away from his embrace. She patted the chair next to her.

"Let's make some plans. When, how, where?"

He looked at her with questions in his eyes.

"Where can we get married?"

"There's a chaplain at Fort Robinson and the Episcopal Church at Pine Ridge."

"Where would we live? Would we have to live in a tepee? I noticed there are some houses where Dove teaches. That wouldn't be so bad."

"We won't go to Pine Ridge, but to my tribe, Big Foot's band. There are houses, but I would like to live in a tepee like my fathers."

"What would you do? It isn't a matter of money—as I told you, I've plenty, but you must have something to do. You've learned to work—I wouldn't want to see you loafing around like the other men."

"According to the last treaty, all male Indians will be given some land. I think I could till the soil."

Brenna considered the few days she'd spent in Sitting Bull's camp. Could she live out her existence in such a place?

Noting the look of happiness on his face, she couldn't let Brown know the doubts that filtered through her mind. She pulled his head down and kissed him lightly on the lips, and at that moment, Kirby and Stuart walked into the parlor. Brenna took one look at the blood draining from Kirby's face, and she didn't look at him again.

"We will be married," Brown explained, "and move to the reservation."

Kirby's voice sounded strained, and he labored under obvious emotion when he spoke. "You're both crazy. This talk about the White Buffalo Calf Maiden is nothing but a myth."

He dropped to his knees in front of Brenna and turned her face toward him. "Listen to me. Please don't let him force you into this. You'll be miserable. Your life will be ruined."

He held her face so she couldn't turn away, but she lowered her eyelids. She couldn't look at his face when she told him. "He didn't force me. I'm sorry, Kirby, but I love him. I don't welcome the hardships of such a marriage, but I'm content to go with him."

"But you're used to his acting like one of us. He won't be like that if he goes back to the reservation. He'll be a Sioux there."

Unbidden, there came to Brenna's mind Brown's actions at the Sioux camp, how he'd left all the hard work to Dove and her. Chances are, Dove wouldn't be around, so guess who'd be putting up the tepee, and doing all the cooking?

"I expect that."

Kirby whirled away and stomped around the room. "I can't believe it. Both of you throwing your lives away. It's going to be downhill all the way for the Sioux now. Can't you see that?"

He turned to Stuart. "You talk some sense to her. She's your daughter."

Stuart's face was sober. "Yes, but she's also her mother's daughter. I told Brenna this morning that it would be a mistake, but she has to make the decision."

"Then if you must marry, stay here," Kirby tried once more. "It won't be a good arrangement for me, but I can accept that better than to see the two of you bury yourselves on a reservation."

Brenna looked hopefully at Brown, but his face was stolid, unrelenting.

"I would prefer that, of course. I have that money Stuart gave the Andersons, and we could use that to start a cattle ranch."

"The *piedra de toque* should go back to the reservation. I want to take it there," Brown said.

"And right or wrong, I'm going where he wants to go."

Kirby took his defeat like a man. He shook hands with

Brown and kissed Brenna on the cheek. "Then I hope you'll find happiness," he said in a trembling voice.

He hurried out of the room, and as his boots clumped down the porch steps, Brenna momentarily panicked. Had she really turned down the man she'd dreamed about for three years?

11

*B*renna had hoped that they would be gone before Mendy returned from her honeymoon, but three days before she and Brown planned to leave, Mendy and Ike returned, giggling and gushing like a couple of youngsters. Brenna waited until the newlyweds settled into the little cabin Kirby provided them before she told Mendy about her plans. Then in addition to Kirby's anger and disappointment and Stuart's disapproval, she had to put up with Mendy's scolding.

"Missy, are you out of yore mind? You cain't go out there and live in a tent. Miz Susan will raise up out of her grave. I thought you wanted Mistah Kirby."

Brenda flushed. "I *am* going, so you mind your own business. When you took a notion to get married, you didn't think it was necessary to consult me."

"But you and me are different. You've got that big house back in Philadelphia, and with a crook of yore finger, you could live in this one right here. Why go off half-cocked and marry an Injun and go to live in a tent? You're crazy."

"Stop calling it a tent—it's a tepee."

"If you go, I'm goin', too."

"You *can't* go. You're married now, remember."

Since Stuart had made arrangements for them to be married at Fort Robinson, Brenna thought she probably should have invited everyone at the Bar C, but she couldn't bear to have Kirby at her wedding. Seeing him walk around the house as though he'd been to a funeral unnerved her enough, so they asked only Stuart and White Dove to be with them.

Upon Kirby's insistence, Brown had finally agreed to take a wagon and team, some farming implements, as well as Raindrop and Midnight for their saddle horses. Stuart and Tatoke saw to it that the wagon contained food, bedding, and other household items.

When Brown protested, Stuart turned on him angrily. "Do you realize what it's going to be like for Brenna to live in a Sioux camp? She has no idea herself, and the reality may be more than she can handle. You'd better let us give you anything that can possibly make her life bearable."

Brown turned startled eyes upon Stuart, and that night he sought Brenna out. "Want to call it off?" he asked.

Deep down inside her, a voice cried, "Yes, yes," but she loved this man, and she wouldn't hurt him. If he would only forget his vision, his need to return to the reservation, and start ranching, she could be happy with him, but when she remembered how life had been at Sitting Bull's camp, she didn't see how she would be able to stand its rigors.

"Of course, I don't want to call it off! Are *you* trying to back out?"

The light in his eyes repaid her for the lie she'd forced past her lips, and she must have been convincing, because he didn't argue further. He kissed her lightly—his eyes promising more later.

Brenna felt like slapping Mendy as she helped her dress the next day. Tears ran down the black woman's face, and occasionally she'd let out a loud wail, but Brenna tried to ignore her. She knew Mendy would be lost without her, but the woman's grief didn't make it any easier.

Despite how she might look in a few months, Brenna determined to look her best today. She decided to wear the white buckskin garment. Her only jewelry would be the touchstone. After Mendy brushed her long hair until it gleamed, allowing it to flow over her shoulders, Brenna placed a leather headband around her forehead and admitted she looked enough like a Sioux to be taken for the White Buffalo Calf Maiden.

Answering a tap at the door, Mendy said, "Good morning, Mistah Kirby," and Brenna's heartbeat faltered. She turned to face him, but he stayed on the threshold, his blue eyes taking in the picture she made. She vividly remembered when she'd first seen him standing in front of the Anderson's door in Philadelphia.

"I can't bear to be here when you leave, so I'm heading out on the range, but I want you to promise that you'll let me know if there's anything I can do to help you. Brown is too proud to ask for help, so I'm appealing to you."

"That's good of you, Kirby, when I've treated you shabbily."

He waved away her words. "That makes no difference. I still feel the same way about you, and I'm worried about the unrest among the Sioux. Promise me."

Brenna smiled slightly. "I promise, but I'm sure we'll be all right."

He entered the room then, and drew her into his arms. She didn't protest. How could she deny him that? His body trembled as she raised her face. He kissed her longingly, and it was a terrible moment for both of them.

"I love you, Brenna. Whatever happens, I want you to know you'll always have a home at the Bar C."

He bolted out of the room as if all the demons of hell were

on his trail, and as his steps receded down the hall Mendy sobbed wildly.

Brenna turned angrily toward her. "Stop it! Stop it, I say. I'm determined not to shed any tears on my wedding day, and if you keep that up, I'll be bawling, too. I'm not going to Brown with red eyes, so stop it."

"Yes, missy."

The bad moment passed, and as soon as she heard Kirby's horse canter away from the stable Brenna hurried downstairs on light feet and with a lighter heart.

Brown awaited her on the porch, and he appraised her garments approvingly. He wore a new set of buckskins and moccasins, and a beaded band held back his shoulder-length hair. She reached her hand to him, and he squeezed it tightly. He lifted a bouquet of sweet peas from the swing and handed them to her. "As sweet as you."

"I love you," she whispered, and only then did she become aware of Stuart and White Dove standing behind her.

"Let's go," Brown said, and he stood aside to let Brenna precede him down the steps to the loaded wagon. That bit of courtesy encouraged her. When they reached the reservation, he might revert to Sioux ways, but here, at least, he continued to observe the amenities of her culture.

They had chosen to have the ceremony outside the fort's buildings, gathering under a cottonwood tree. Colonel Henry came by to wish them happiness, but Brenna considered it a halfhearted wish. The chaplain obviously performed the service through coercion from his superiors, and she figured that her connection with the Bar C provided the only reason the officers had agreed to have the ceremony at the fort. But when she asked Colonel Henry if the camp photographer would take their picture, he agreed, and refused the coins she offered in payment.

"Consider it a wedding gift," Henry said. "We'll send the photograph to the Bar C when it's developed."

After the brief ceremony, Stuart kissed her. "Guess I might as well take my rights as father of the bride," he said, which earned him a disapproving look from the chaplain.

Stuart shook hands with Brown and said meaningfully, "Don't forget what a jewel you're getting today, and I don't mean the *piedra de toque.* If we can ever help you, don't be too proud to ask us. Come in often to see us anyway."

Brown nodded agreement, and then they were on their way. Brenna turned to wave at Stuart and Dove, then resolutely turned forward and refused to look back again. She was a Sioux wife now, and she needed to remember that.

"How far away will we be from the Bar C?"

"By wagon, a week, eight days mebbe. Quicker on horseback. No hurry now. What say, want a honeymoon?"

"I say, good idea." He stopped the horses and drew her into his arms. Before his lips dropped to hers, she whispered, "Be sure you have hold of the reins—remember what happened that day in the snow."

"I remember—nothing compared to what will happen today."

The trail Brown followed led upward through tree-covered hills, fresh with the scent of pine and wildflowers, and late in the evening, he drove into a secluded area in a small canyon. High walls rose on each side of a gurgling creek flowing over round boulders. Cottonwood and willow trees grew along its banks, and green grass carpeted the valley. A herd of antelope grazed not far from where Brown stopped the wagon.

"Beautiful!"

His eyes gleamed with pride that he'd found a place to please her.

"Be nice if we could stay here forever." She wished immediately that she could recall the words, for his eyes clouded.

"Not long. Have a duty to the Sioux."

"I'll just enjoy it as long as I'm here." She jumped down without his help. "And just to show you that I'm determined to make you a good wife, I'm going to help set up camp."

"Not necessary till we join our people," he said as he started to unload the wagon.

"I'd better start learning now. I don't want you to be ashamed of me."

"I won't be."

Brown set up the small tent, and Brenna helped him, although she reasoned he could probably have done it faster without her help. He built a fire, and Brenna started cooking the meal, but when she upended the ham into the flames, she sat down.

"Maybe I had better watch, until I get the hang of it."

He smiled at her. "Fetch water, if you want to help. There's a bucket in the wagon."

She marveled at how quickly he prepared the food—ham, potatoes, and biscuits. He reached in the wagon. "My mother sent cake and pickles."

Brenna did wash the pans, and then they sat holding hands as the darkness shadowed their surroundings. Stars crept into view over their heads, a full moon peeped over the canyon wall.

"Let's spread our blankets out here," Brenna said. "The night's too beautiful to sleep under the tent."

"Good idea," Brown agreed, and he brought bed rolls from the wagon, placed them together, and spread a blanket over the top.

Brenna could never remember afterward if she slept at all that night, but when daylight started creeping into the canyon, Brown still slept, and Brenna contemplated what had happened to them. They weren't individuals anymore; they had been joined into one entity. She wondered why so little was said about the beauty of marrying one's body to another, but she supposed the experience couldn't be put into mere words. She sighed deeply, and the sound awakened her husband.

He raised on one elbow and peered down at her face in the first blush of dawn. His eyes asked a question.

"Yes," Brenna murmured. "I love you. Wherever you go, whatever you do, I'm yours until death separates us."

"Didn't want you to be sorry. To go with me will not always be good, but I'll make it as easy as I can."

Brown seemed in no hurry to reach his destination, and they dawdled along the trail. The hours turned into one long honeymoon. They didn't talk a great deal, and when they did, it was always about the past.

But on the tenth day after they left the Bar C, when they awakened, Brown said, "Put on the white garment and the *piedra de toque* today," and Brenna's pulse quickened. A few hours later, Brown stopped the team on top of a ridge, and when Brenna saw the many tepees scattered around a stream in the valley below, she thought, *The honeymoon is over. Real life begins now.*

Her hands clasped the touchstone. *If you do have any power, I need a lot of it now.* It gave her no assurance, and she admitted that it was only an inanimate object after all. So she prayed, "Jesus, You're *my* touchstone. You're the one who paved the way to a beautiful life. While I'm here in this village, help me to point these people to You."

When Brown released the brake and eased the wagon carefully down the steep bank, Brenna touched his arm. His hands were busy with the horses, but he flashed her a look of understanding that brought her reassurance.

Their entrance into the village caused little excitement, except for the dogs that yapped noisily and nipped at the horses' hooves. Brown guided the wagon toward the largest tepee, and when he stopped the team, the flap opened, and a tall, spare man stepped out.

"Big Foot," Brown murmured. No doubt, at one time Big Foot had been an admirable figure of a man, but his lusterless eyes were deep set, and his skin stretched tightly over a bony, angular face. In spite of the frailness of his body, he exhibited a regal bearing.

Brown lifted his hand in greeting, and Big Foot returned the salute. Her husband laid his hand on Brenna's leg before he stepped from the wagon and addressed the chief in his own language.

She didn't understand a thing they said to each other, even though she'd picked up a few words in Sitting Bull's camp, and she made up her mind she would learn the Sioux language. If she were destined to live here, she wanted to communicate with her neighbors.

"Come," Brown said, interrupting her reverie. He helped her from the wagon and stood back to let her precede him into the tepee, actions no Sioux would have normally accorded his wife, and she realized Brown had meant what he said about making life as easy as possible for her.

Smoke from the firepit on the floor of the tepee stung Brenna's eyes as it drifted toward smoke wings at the top of the pole framework. A lining of skins surrounded the walls. Beds of grass padding covered with buffalo robes and skins lay around the walls, and items of clothing and cooking utensils hung from the lodge poles.

Big Foot sat on a tattered buffalo skin, and he motioned Brown and Brenna to a seat near him. The chief lifted a feathered pipe and held it while a woman took a small coal from the fire pit and lighted the pipe, before she disappeared out the door flap. A buffalo calf had been carved on the red stone bowl, and twelve feathers hung from the wooden stem.

Big Foot sucked noisily on the pipe and handed it to

Brown. Brenna feared she might be expected to smoke the odorous thing, but after the two men exchanged the pipe between them several times, Big Foot laid it aside.

The chief waved his hand toward Brown, who started talking slowly in Sioux, but after each pause, he quickly translated his words to Brenna.

"I am Brown Bear, Miniconjou by birth, but for several years, I've lived among the white men. I went from my tribe many seasons ago to Carlisle Indian School."

Big Foot nodded.

"My squaw," and he gave Brenna an apologetic look, "is a mixed blood, but her mother, Santee, was a kinsman of Big Foot. In the Moon of Making Fat, I, Brown, attended the sun dance in the camp of Sitting Bull. The Great Spirit told me soon the White Buffalo Calf Maiden would return to the Sioux and that I would have the sign to know when she came. The daughter of Santee has for many moons lived in the Great Father's land," he waved his hand toward the east, "and only in the Moon of the Snowblind did she come to this country. She brought with her the sign I looked for, the *piedra de toque*."

He removed the touchstone from Brenna's neck and dangled it before Big Foot's eyes. "My Brenna bears the sign; she is the White Buffalo Calf Maiden returned to the Sioux."

Big Foot's hand trembled as he grasped the *piedra de toque*. "I have not seen it before. Long have I heard tales of it, but the bearer of the stone always keeps it secret, or the magic will not work. Because of ill fortune of the Sioux, I know the *piedra de toque* must be gone, but now it is returned to my people."

The look of hope that touched the old man's face distressed Brenna, and she wanted to cry out, "Don't base your hope on me or that necklace. There's nothing supernatural about either of us."

"Because of the trials of my people, we have come to live with Big Foot and his band."

Big Foot turned his gaze toward Brenna. "Stand, please," he said in English.

"Are you the Buffalo Calf Maiden?" he demanded.

Brown's eyes flashed a warning.

"I do not know. The Great Spirit did not reveal my Sioux heritage to me until a few moons ago. But since I have the *piedra de toque* in my possession, I have come to cast my lot with the Miniconjou."

Brenna was right proud of that speech, and Brown must have been, too, for he threw her a grateful glance.

"You look like the maiden," Big Foot said in his broken English, "tall, fair, and beautiful." Then he turned to Brown, "My son, I do not doubt your vision, but we must be sure. A new day is dawning for the Sioux, and at this moment, great things are happening on the reservation. For the moment, we will not spread the news that the maiden has returned. When good fortune returns to the Miniconjou, we will know your sign is true, and we will send the maiden throughout the Sioux nation. Keep your counsel about the maiden and the *piedra de toque*." He returned the necklace to Brenna.

"Then we may dwell with Big Foot?" Brown asked.

"Be at peace with us, my son."

Brown held back the flap for Brenna to leave, and sunlight pierced her eyes after the darkness of the tepee. They climbed into the wagon, and Brown drove upstream from Big Foot's lodge. Passing the last tepee, he traveled a quarter of a mile before he stopped.

"Too close?"

Brenna kissed him gratefully. "This is fine." She hadn't even had to voice her desire for privacy; he'd understood.

Green grass lined the creek bank, and the gurgle of water flowing over a few rocks lent a peaceful air to the spot. She thought Brown's choice had been made because he understood that she wouldn't want close confinement with the others, but when he lifted her from the wagon and pulled her close, she sensed immediately the depth of his desire for her, making her wonder if the choice of an isolated spot had been made for him as much as for herself.

"I'll put up the tepee now."

"Is this the same one we used at Sitting Bull's camp?" she asked, wondering if she would be expected to erect the structure by herself. But Brown did most of the work, while she puttered around in his way, looking busy.

On the trail, Brenna had watched while Brown made preparations for the night, but today her life as a Sioux woman had to start. While Brown unloaded their possessions, with clumsy fingers, Brenna gathered wood and started a fire. She found a bucket in the wagon and carried water from the creek, thankful that being upstream from the main camp would provide them purer water.

"As dry as the countryside is, I'm surprised that there's any water in this river," she said when she panted up to Brown, with water sloshing over the sides of the bucket.

"Fed from underground," he said. "Get some of the dried beef Tatoke sent, and put onions and potatoes in the pot with it. Keep water in the pot and the fire low. Takes a long time to cook supper. We'll only eat two times here in camp."

By the time Brenna had the stew ready to serve, grime smeared her face, two fingers had painful burns, and her arms bore smoke streaks. *At this rate, I won't have any time to write a book,* she thought ruefully. Brown had come to her rescue by making a pan of bread and the coffee, or they wouldn't have had enough to eat.

In spite of her inexperience, the food tasted good enough, and they ate heartily. *Maybe I'll make it after all,* she thought wearily as she crawled under the blankets into Brown's warm embrace, but the weariness left her body in the wake of his caresses, and she stretched in his arms.

"Sorry you came with me?" he whispered, his lips on hers, seeking his own reassurance.

She lifted her lips long enough to murmur, "What do you think?"

12

"*B*rown, there's no way you can farm this land," Brenna exclaimed after several rides around the Cheyenne River reservation. The burning sun and hot winds withered fields of corn. A few gardens showed little reward for the natives' efforts. Bean leaves curled and turned brown. Cabbage heads were no bigger than apples. Pumpkin vines lay wilted and lifeless.

"How can the government expect the Indians to become farmers when they shove them onto land like this?"

Brown shrugged his shoulders and didn't answer. In the month they'd lived in Big Foot's camp, Brenna had noted a change in Brown, as if he were accepting the hopelessness of their situation. His despondency made Brenna more determined that his vision would come to fulfillment.

"Could we graze cattle, do you think?"

"Mebbe. There's some grass and water."

"Will you let me buy some cattle? You must have something to do."

"Don't want to spend your money. Got a little myself."

"It's *our* money now. Don't you understand? When I married you, we became one."

A look of interest flitted across Brown's face, and he gazed around. "Mebbe start with twenty, thirty head, and if they do well, we could increase the herd. Might be the answer for the Sioux. How do we get them?"

"From the Bar C, of course. Kirby will be glad to help us. I'll write him a letter about what we want and how to receive credit from my bank in Philadelphia. Will you take the letter?"

"No, we'll send one of the men. I won't leave you here by yourself."

Knowing it would be several weeks before the cattle could arrive, Brenna set herself to learning Sioux ways. They'd brought plenty of provisions with them, and Brown had asked fourteen-year-old Bright Star to help Brenna.

Bright Star's mother had made Brenna two buckskin outfits that she wore around the cooking fire, but every evening she put on one of her dresses. She felt determined not to become lax in her personal appearance, and after their work was over for the day, she'd have Bright Star or Brown stand guard while she bathed in the creek and washed her hair.

Brown kept his tidy appearance, too, and the extra washing she did to keep them that way was worth it. When the tribe went to the agency for their monthly rations, Brenna went along, because she wanted to see the government issue firsthand and to buy some serviceable clothes for them. She had no trouble finding flannel shirts and pants for Brown, but she balked at the gaudy calico dresses.

"Do they think all Indian women are the same size?" she demanded of the clerk. "And why such ugly garments?"

The clerk looked her over impudently. "The Indians like 'em."

Brenna also checked into the rations the Indians received

and seethed with indignation. Musty beans, rancid smoked meat, and weevilly flour constituted the largest portion of food. Ginger snaps were spongy to the touch. The only things fit to eat were the canned items.

The agent obviously didn't like her snooping around and became indignant when he saw her taking notes. She made up her mind right then that she'd send some correspondence East in a hurry.

She fumed about the situation all the way back to camp, until Brown said, "Don't get worked up about it. You can write, but nothing'll be done. White people don't care about Sioux."

"I'm not going to give up anyway. I know several of Dad's friends who might have some influence."

"If you want to get mad, I'll tell you something worse. When the government broke up Big Reservation last year, they gave each Indian a farm. So the Great White Father felt generous to give Indian what is already his. Got all the Indian had to give and decided to cut rations. If Indians own land now, they can farm and raise their own food. Beef rations are only half as much as last year—ask Kirby, he will tell you the Bar C sells only half what they did last year."

"But nobody can raise food on this land. It's worthless for farming."

"Don't tell me—tell Congress, which doesn't know or care." He shook his head. "Last winter lots of babies died from measles, whooping cough—it'll be worse this season."

Sharing his burden brought a wave of emotion over her, and Brenna said softly, "There's one Sioux this white woman cares about."

"Who? Big Foot?" His eyes teased her.

"Guess again."

Brown pulled Midnight close to her and took her hand. "Shouldn't have brought you here. But I had a great love for you, and it grows more and more each day." He touched his chest. "Sometimes this heart is so full of love I think it will explode."

Tears misted Brenna's eyes. "I wouldn't have it any other way. I love you, too. I'm just thankful I was wise enough to follow my heart."

"But promise me, if anything happens to me, you'll go back to Kirby at Bar C. He and Stuart will look after you."

To ease his burden, she said, "I promise."

With Bright Star and Brown coaching her, in a few weeks, Brenna had gained an adequate command of the language to circulate among the people.

At seminary, Brenna had learned some sewing, so she taught Bright Star and the other young women how to turn the gaudy calico into usable garments. While they sewed, Brenna talked to them of her Christian faith. Sometimes she read to them from the Bible. They liked to hear her read, but she wondered if they comprehended the real meaning of the words.

At times, Brenna questioned if she might *be* the White Buffalo Calf Maiden, and she figured that Brown and Big Foot often pondered the same thing, for she had brought some comfort and help to the Miniconjou.

The old chief's eyes followed her approvingly as she moved among his people, and often she stopped to visit him as he sat outside his tepee. Big Foot's health had deteriorated in the few weeks she'd been here, and observing the bloody spittle around his tepee, she deduced he must have tuberculosis.

In spite of his broken English and her small knowledge of Sioux, from Big Foot Brenna gained a greater knowledge of the downfall of her husband's people. She filled her notebooks rapidly.

One day the chief surprised her by saying, "Maiden, I have liked your presence among us, but it would have been better for your young warrior if he had stayed with the whites."

"But he'd had the vision, and he would never have been happy without fulfilling that command from *Wakantanka*."

"I, too, have had my visions, but they are no more. Soon I will go to my fathers." He lifted a weak, emaciated arm. "Once Big Foot was the strongest of his tribe. I climbed to a high peak of the mountains." He gestured westward. "There *Wakantanka* revealed that I would be a leader of my people."

"And you have. Your people respect you very much."

He bowed his head. "Why should they? I have not been able to keep the white man from taking our lands. Everything is gone—our sacred hills, our way of life. No means of living except to take the bounty of the white man. I have failed. When I enter the hunting grounds in the great beyond, I will not stand like a man before my ancestors. I have failed them as well as the people I lead."

Brenna took his shaking hands between hers. "It is not so. No one could have done better than you. Americans are possessed with the desire to conquer this continent, and many of them honestly think that the Sioux would be better off to live the white man's way."

"But we do not want their culture, and we have fought to keep our way of life."

"You put up a brave fight, but the whites are too many for you. If the Sioux wiped out every white in Sioux country, there would still be a never-ending tide to take their place."

"Yes, Sitting Bull of the Hunkpapas has told me of the big cities, of the people so numerous that they looked like ants crawling around their rock streets. Hearing that, I lost heart. I no longer wish to fight, simply to save the lives of my tribe."

Brenna walked back to their tepee, her thoughts in turmoil. She certainly had plenty of information for a book, but if she wrote the bold truth, would she ever find a publisher? She had to try, she must do something to help her people. *Her* people? Living in two worlds, she hardly knew where her loyalties lay.

The Sioux could benefit from the white culture: more comfortable housing, education, travel. But considering the Sioux's love for the land, their respect for tribal unity, and their reverence for the Great Spirit, wouldn't it take generations before they could adopt white ways?

The next day while they washed garments in the creek, Brenna noticed that Bright Star kept glancing westward, with a dreamy look in her eyes. This wasn't the first time Brenna had noted the girl's action, and she finally asked, "Who are you always looking for? Some young brave who'll take you to his tepee?"

"No, more important than a brave. Kicking Bear should return soon."

Brenna had heard his name mentioned before, but she hadn't seen him. "Is he one of your medicine men?"

"He is a kinsman of Big Foot. Many moons ago he traveled west of mountains, and he brought good news to share with the Sioux. All this season he has taught a new dance to our brothers; soon we will be dancing here."

Brenna scrubbed harder on the back of Brown's shirt. "What do you mean?"

"The Sioux now have a new religion where Sioux come back to life and white men disappear. Big Foot's been slow to believe, but soon Kicking Bear will come to teach our band to dance."

Could this be the ghost dance Brenna had heard mentioned at the Bar C?

That evening, after supper, Brown saddled their horses, and as they traveled eastward, Brenna thought of Bright Star's remarks. "Brown, what's all this about Big Foot's people starting to dance in a new religion? What do you know about it?"

"Enough to know I don't like it. A Paiute shaman's supposed to have visited the Great Spirit in heaven. He learned about a time when the buffalo again will fill the plains and dead tribesmen will come to life."

"Kicking Bear believed that?"

"Yes, it's supposed to happen when the Indians learn a dance that will make the white man disappear. Kicking Bear's been traveling among the Sioux all summer, teaching the new dance."

After they traveled several miles, Brown stopped his horse in a secluded glen. Brenna feasted her eyes on the most pleasant sight she'd seen since her arrival on the reservation.

"Like it?" Brown's eyes watched her anxiously.

"Yes. It's beautiful."

"Mebbe we should build a home here. Each Sioux's supposed to have land from government. Nobody else has taken this yet. I'll get it for us."

Her eyes lighted. "Oh, yes. We could graze cattle here. You would still be living on the reservation, but we could have a ranch of our own."

He lifted her off the horse, and they strolled around the glade, choosing a place for their house and other buildings, dreaming the hours away. As the shadows lengthened Brown sat on the ground and pulled her into his arms. Basking in his warmth as well as the rays of the sun, half asleep, Brenna murmured, "Are you going to learn that new dance?"

"No. The dance is supposed to bring back Indians but cover up all whites. You're too much white; I don't want to lose you."

"Wonder why?" she teased as she leaned over and kissed him.

*   *   *

The next afternoon, Bright Star came running toward Brenna. "Cows coming. Lots of cowboys. Wagons," the girl called.

Brenna had hardly dared to hope Kirby would send the cattle to them so soon, even though the messenger they'd sent to the Bar C had been back in camp for several days. Hearing a running horse, she looked out to see Brown waving at her.

"Cattle coming. I'll ride out to meet them."

Cattle bawled, and camp dogs were barking, so Brenna hurried outside just as a wagon halted in front of their tepee. She hardly noticed that Stuart King was driving, because her eyes lighted on his companion.

"Mendy!" she screamed and ran to the wagon. Mendy clambered down over the wheel more quickly than her girth warranted, and she snatched Brenna into a tight embrace.

"My child!"

"Mendy, you came to see me!" Tears welled in her eyes, and she blinked rapidly.

"Had to see with my own eyes where you'd taken yourself, and I've suffered perdition, hell, and the grave riding up here in that wagon."

"I tried to warn her it wasn't an easy trip, but she was bound to come," Stuart said.

Brenna turned to him. "Oh, I'm glad to see all of you." She threw her arms around Stuart, and he held her at arm's length for a better look.

"I've never thought so before, but you look like your mother today."

A wistful note crept into his voice, and Brenna looked keenly at him. "You loved her? Were happy with her?"

He nodded toward the tepee. "We lived in a place like that for a few years before I went back to the Bar C."

Brenna heard a step behind her, and she whirled, thinking

it was Brown. Kirby stood there, his blue eyes alight with pleasure.

"Have you saved any of that hugging for me?"

More diffident than she'd been with Stuart and Mendy, Brenna held out her arms, and Kirby pulled her close. To still the pounding of her heart, she said lightly, "Say, who's minding the Bar C, with all of you up here?"

"Guess we left White Dove in charge."

"Oh, I'm happy you came. Eat supper with us. I want to show you I've learned to cook."

They pulled the bed wagon up beside the tepee, then left to corral the cattle, and Mendy began unloading items.

"Didn't suppose you'd have anything to eat, so I brought some things. There's a smoked ham in here and some of Tatoke's bread. I even made some pies, which I kept hidden all the way, so the cowboys wouldn't smell them."

Laughing happily, Brenna said, "I'll be glad to have some of your cooking, but tonight you're going to eat what I prepared. Good thing I made a big pan of corn bread."

Stuart strolled into camp and hunkered beside the tepee. "Just fix for Kirby and me. The other boys will eat at the chuckwagon and keep the cattle settled."

"Where's my husband anyway?"

"He's coming with Kirby. Kirby stopped to pay his respects to Big Foot."

When the two men arrived, Brenna said, "Supper's ready, but don't expect a feast. If I'd known all of you were coming, I could have prepared some more."

Brown lifted the heavy pot from the tripod, then stooped to uncover the iron skillet that held the corn pone—actions she hoped didn't escape the attention of Kirby and Stuart. She wanted them to see that Brown cherished and cared for her.

She handed around the bowls of beans, and corn bread, and Brown removed the roasting pheasants from the spits he'd made for her. "Not many pheasants around here. Lucky to find these two yesterday."

"Lucky for us," Stuart commented as he tore off chunks of a drumstick with his teeth. "You've had a good teacher, Brenna; this food is good."

Brenna coveted Kirby's approval, which wasn't long coming. His eyes glowed tenderly, and he said, "You amaze me, Brenna. I believe you'd have made a good pioneer woman."

One pheasant and the beans disappeared in a hurry. "We were going to have canned peaches for dessert, or would you rather have some of Mendy's pies?"

"Pies?" Stuart and Kirby shouted in unison.

"Have you been holding out on us?" Kirby added.

Mendy switched her skirts impudently as she went to the wagon and lifted out two huckleberry pies. "They might be a little stale, but least I got here with 'em, which I wouldn't have did if you cowboys had known about 'em."

"Uh-huh!" Stuart said. "What say, Kirby? Let's just drop this little woman somewhere along the trail on the way back home."

Mendy giggled wickedly. "You jest do that, Mistah Stuart, and you'll have my Ike to deal with."

"How long are you going to be here?" Brenna asked, when Kirby and Stuart started to head back to the cow camp.

"We'll just lay over one day to give the horses time to rest up. We start home at dawn, day after tomorrow," Kirby answered.

Mendy helped with cleaning up the utensils, and as soon as she went into the wagon, Brenna and Brown sought their own bed. He pulled her close and kissed the lowest part of her neck. She sighed deeply.

"Happy?"

"Yes, but I was happy before they came. If I'm with you, I'm contented."

After Brown left the next morning, Kirby soon arrived at

the tepee. "Let's take a walk, shall we?" They went a short distance up the creek and sat on the bank in full view of the camp.

"Did you receive credit from my bank for the cows?"

"I didn't try." He held up one hand. "Now, let me explain. I consider that Brown is due something from the Bar C. Father left everything to me, with no interest to Tatoke. She refused to accept anything from me, so let's consider these cows a payment on her inheritance."

"However you like, but I can afford to pay for them. Do you think it will work, Kirby?" She turned anxious brown eyes toward him. "Can he raise cattle here?"

"Probably, if the rains come, but there hasn't been much rain, and even my range land is drying up. I may have to sell off cattle earlier than I usually do."

"I suggested trying to raise cattle when I realized there's no way to farm this land. Every time I look around this reservation, I grow furious to know how the government has cheated these people."

"It won't get any better," Kirby warned. "I'm worried about your being up here. These Indians can become hostile overnight. I can't say I'm reconciled to having you married to him, but I could accept it better if I knew you were safe. I wish Brown would come back to the Bar C."

"I wish so, too, but I'm going to stay with him. I have enough of that money Stuart gave to my father so we could start a ranch, and I'm sure he would like that. If the Sioux were prospering, I think he'd leave, but when their life is so hard, he feels guilty not to share it."

"Then is there anything I can do for you?"

"Not now. Brown is going to build a house, and when I see what I need for it, perhaps I can send you a list, and you can order it for me. He's trying so hard to make my life bearable."

Kirby searched her face, and what he saw there must have

made him finally accept that he had lost her, for a look of resignation filtered into his eyes. "I guess I should just tend to my own business, for obviously you're happy with him." They started slowly toward the tepee.

How could she possibly ease the hurt Kirby must feel? How could she let him know of the high regard she had for him without being disloyal to Brown? He had been careful not to touch her, and when she took his hand, she felt him tremble.

"Kirby, I only wish there were two of me—that I had two hearts to give. But since I have only one, I couldn't divide it, and it had to be Brown's, perhaps because he needs me so much more."

He squeezed her hand and released it. "I understand, my dear. You see, I love him, too; he's been a true brother to me."

Brenna watched the Bar C outfit pull out the next morning, barely able to restrain her tears. She'd be much more lonely now, and perhaps Brown sensed this, for he promised Stuart, "We'll come for a visit soon."

13

*B*eating drums awakened Brenna, but nippy morning air penetrated the tepee, and she curled closer to Brown for warmth. She sat up, startled, for Brown no longer lay beside her. What could have happened? He never left their bed without pulling her into a tight embrace and kissing her.

The drumbeats increased in volume, and a strange sense of foreboding swept over Brenna. She threw back the blankets, shivering as she hurried into her clothes. The Moon When the Calves Grow Hair, plain old September to her, was almost gone, and frost had come early, killing the few crops that had survived the drought of summer. Surely by now Brown must know that she wasn't the White Buffalo Calf Maiden.

Pulling a cloak around her, Brenna started to look for Brown, but he opened the flap and entered the tepee.

"What's going on?"

"The drums woke me. I went to find out what they mean." He paused, and Brenna waited breathlessly. "Kicking Bear and Short Bull have come into camp."

"Have they started that crazy dancing?"

"Not yet. Big Foot called a council meeting at noon. Let's cook food now. I want to be at the council."

"Will I be allowed to listen?"

He nodded and went outside to start the fire. "Cold this morning."

Big Foot's whole band must have assembled, Brenna decided when she and Brown left their tepee at noon. A large group sat on the ground behind the dwellings, and a man whom Brenna took to be Kicking Bear stood on the knoll above them. A tall Sioux with a stern face, he had buffalo horns on his head, with several leaves stuck in his headband. His eyes displayed a faraway, mystical expression.

As she and Brown sat down among the people, Brenna was reminded of a picture she'd seen of Jesus teaching on the mount. The people's uplifted faces fastened on Kicking Bear, hope showing in their eyes, waiting to hear that their lives would improve.

"Lord," she prayed, "this is all so futile. If only they could trust in You!"

Kicking Bear stood, animated face uplifted, and then he started shuffling his feet, moving in a counterclockwise circle, chanting words that Brenna couldn't understand. Big Foot labored up the little hill, his breath coming in short gasps. He sat on a rock until Kicking Bear stopped the shuffling and chanting.

Big Foot stood and addressed his people. "Kicking Bear has a strange tale to tell us that he shared with other Sioux. We will listen."

For a few minutes Kicking Bear silently surveyed his audience, and then he started talking in a slow monotone that Brenna could follow.

"Many moons ago, word came to the Sioux of the ghost dance, a new religion started by the Paiute messiah Wovoka. In the Moon When Ponies Shed, with others of my tribe, I started a long journey across the mountains. We rode on the white man's iron horse.

"When the iron horse ran out, two Indians met us, gave us meat, bread, and horses, and guided us on a trail that took four suns. There we came to a village of fish eaters, near a great lake. The fish eaters said that the messiah had returned to earth and that he had sent for us."

Suddenly Kicking Bear appeared to go into a trance, and he spent fifteen minutes or more going through the shuffling dance again. Despite the cold wind, heat suffused Brenna's body, and she felt faint. She moved closer to Brown so she could touch him. He flashed an understanding glance toward her, and she felt comfortable enough to take some interest in their companions. The rapt expressions on the faces of these people disturbed her. Another man joined Kicking Bear, and the dancing continued. Several people in the audience started to weave back and forth, but Kicking Bear stopped dancing, slumped on the ground, and continued his narrative.

"Then we moved on to Walker Lake, where we waited for two days with hundreds of other Indians from many different reservations, some speaking tongues strange to us. The messiah had sent for them, too.

"Just before sundown on the third day, the messiah appeared. Always before I thought the messiah was a white man, but this man looked like an Indian. He said, 'I want to talk to you about your dead relatives. I will teach you a new dance.' Then he started to dance, and everybody joined in, the messiah singing while we danced. We danced late into the night."

"If this was the Messiah, did he have the scars the missionaries have talked about?" Big Foot asked.

"There was a scar on his wrist and one on his face, but we couldn't see his feet because of the moccasins he wore. But the words were good. He told us that in the beginning, the

Great Spirit made the earth and then sent his son to the earth to teach people. But the white man had been mean to him, so he had gone back to heaven. Now he's returned as an Indian to make everything the way it used to be."

"When will this happen?" a man sitting beside Brown asked.

"As soon as the Indians learn the new dance, probably by the Moon of the New Grass Appearing. The messiah said we would have a new earth, that the old earth would be covered up. The Indians are to keep dancing so we can stay on top of the dirt."

"But how will this rid us of the white man?"

"Because the white men do not believe, they will be covered up; even Indians who don't believe will perish."

A restlessness stirred the Indians, who until that time had been immobile.

"What language did the messiah speak?" Brown asked.

"I do not know, but I understood his words, as did all the other tribesmen. He used words that all of us knew."

Goose pimples broke out on Brenna's body as she listened. The Sioux were actually looking to Christ for deliverance, but like the Jews of Jesus' day, they expected a militant Christ, one who would deliver them from the oppression of their enemies.

"What do you think of this?" Brenna whispered to her husband.

"Dangerous. My people are without hope—they'll believe anything." He squeezed her hand in a bid for silence.

Kicking Bear spoke again: "We spent a few suns learning the new dance, and we started homeward, the messiah flying above us in the air, teaching us new songs for the dance. When he left us at the railroad, he promised that as soon as winter passes, he will bring the ghosts of our fathers to meet us in a new resurrection."

An old woman in the front row hobbled up the knoll to

stand beside Kicking Bear. Awkwardly she forced her feet to take the steps that Kicking Bear had performed, falling down in the effort. He lifted her to her feet, carefully instructing her how to perform the shuffling dance. Soon dozens of others joined the figures on the mound, and the dust from their shuffling permeated the air until Brenna sneezed.

"Let's go," Brown said.

In a matter of a few days, Big Foot's camp changed from a lethargic community to a village charged with animation and hope. Newcomers poured into the area daily, and almost every morning, Brenna counted new tepees edging close to their home. Most of the newcomers were widows whose husbands had been killed in wars with the whites, and they'd come to learn the dance so they could bring back their deceased spouses.

As tension increased among the Miniconjou, Brown grew more agitated. He wanted to work on the new house, but he hesitated to leave Brenna alone in the encampment. During the next month, the excitement accelerated, until Brenna had the sensation of sitting on a powder keg.

One evening Brown appeared more perturbed than usual, and as they huddled around the fire, he said, "I'm going to take you back to the Bar C for a while."

"Why?"

"Kicking Bear added something to this business I do not like. Wovoka says that the Indians should avoid war, fighting, and that they should not steal, lie, or practice cruelty."

"Not a bad religion for anyone," Brenna reflected.

"Yes, but Kicking Bear adds his own ideas. He has the dancers make special shirts that bullets can't go through."

"Fiddle-faddle! There's no such thing."

"I know, but it scares me anyway. As long as this dancing was nothing more than a religion, it might have escaped notice, but I've lived among whites long enough to know that it won't take them long to start wondering, if this is a peaceful religion, why is it necessary for the Sioux to wear bullet-proof shirts?"

"You think the army will move in?"

He nodded. "Yes, we may have another Indian war, and these shirts will be the end of the Sioux."

"About like the *piedra de toque*, huh?"

"If war comes," Brown said, ignoring her sally about the touchstone, "it's not safe for you here. I'll take you to the Bar C and try to find out what Fort Robinson is doing about this."

"Are you going to stay at the Bar C, too?"

"No, I must be here—can't desert my people now."

"Then I'm not going either. What's happened to your theory that I'm the White Buffalo Calf Maiden, that as bearer of the touchstone, my duty was with the Sioux people?"

He winced a little, and she wished she hadn't had to say it.

"Mebbe I was wrong, I don't know. I do know I want you out of danger."

"Only if you go, too. I would be absolutely miserable wondering what was happening. Please, Brown, I don't want to be stubborn, but I want to stay with you." If he knew her secret, he'd be more determined than ever that she had to leave the reservation, so she didn't tell him the news that she'd been waiting to reveal.

Her words pleased him, and though he still looked worried, he acquiesced. "We see it through together then, but," he took her face between his hands and looked directly into her eyes, "remember the promise you made—and if anything happens to me, you go directly to Bar C."

"I remember, but don't talk like that. Nothing is going to happen to you."

"Mebbe not. If you won't go to Bar C, do write to Kirby. Ask him to find out what Fort Robinson is doing about this ghost dance and send me word. If I can find anyone not dancing, I'll send a messenger."

The next morning when they went out to watch the dancers, sure enough they danced in loose shirts, made out of everything from deerskin to muslin. Some of the garments had been lavishly adorned with feathers, quill work, and painted with mystical designs.

In a few weeks, the Miniconjou had stopped all activity except the ghost dance. All day long and into the night chanting and the shuffling of hundreds of feet echoed through the valley. News filtered into their camp that almost every tribe danced, and Kicking Bear answered an invitation from Sitting Bull to come to his encampment.

Disgusted because he couldn't get anyone to help him with the house, Brown said one day, "There are thousands of people dancing on this reservation, when they should be out hunting game for winter food. Today an old goose honked down to me that it's going to be a cruel winter."

"With the crop failure and this cut in government rations, what will they eat?"

"Hate to say it, but we've only got twenty-four cows now."

"What! You mean they've butchered one of our cows?"

"Looks like it. She could have wandered off, but I doubt it. Too many people in camp."

"The herd won't last long that way. I hate to see the hungry children, but it will take a cow a day to feed these people. Must be five hundred Indians in camp now."

" 'Bout so."

"What does Big Foot think of all this?"

"Same as I do. Wovoka just took part of missionaries religion and mixed it up. Probably fed Kicking Bear, and the others, some locoweed, and they don't know what they saw."

He paused a moment and continued slowly, "Mebbe that's what happened to me at the sun dance. More I see of this, the more I believe the religion I learned at Carlisle. Lived with whites too long to be a good Sioux, I guess."

Brenna waited breathlessly, sensing that Brown might be on the verge of making a decision to return to civilized living. Maybe the war still raged inside him, and she thought desperately, *The Sioux didn't win the war, just a few battles.* She was instantly ashamed of her thoughts.

The choice would have to be his—she wouldn't influence him. But when her stomach quivered, the new life she carried seemed to rebel at the prospect of being born in an Indian tepee, and suddenly she had a clearer understanding of why Stuart had given her into the care of John Anderson.

So intent were they with their own thoughts, they didn't hear the horse ride up to the tepee until a call sounded, "Hello. Anybody home?"

Brown and Brenna exchanged glances. "Kirby?" she said, and Brown moved to open the flap. It *was* Kirby, stepping stiffly from his saddle, wrapped in a sheepskin coat, his sombrero pulled down over his ears.

"Didn't expect you to bring the message yourself," Brown said, as Brenna helped Kirby remove his heavy coat. She poured him a tin cup of coffee from the pot she'd had brewing for their evening meal.

"Wanted to find out for myself what was going on," he said as he stripped off his gloves and held his hands around the warm cup.

"The Sioux have gone crazy," Brenna said.

"What's the army doing?" Brown questioned. "That's what troubles me."

"Nothing right now," Kirby said as he sipped on the warm liquid. "When this news first came in October, the post commander, Colonel Tilford, notified Colonel Royer, the Indian agent at Pine Ridge, that he'd send troops if they were needed. Tilford told me that he thought the Indians could dance as much as they wanted to, as long as they didn't hurt anybody."

"Right now, they hurt nobody but themselves. Pretty hard

to fight soldiers on empty stomachs, and the Sioux have no provisions for winter. Too busy dancing to hunt."

"Little Bat feels the same way as Tilford. You know he has a lot of influence, and he says the ghost dance will die out, if left alone. But Royer is getting nervous about the whole thing, so he came to Fort Robinson for a conference, and a couple of weeks ago the Ninth Cavalry took to the field. Little Bat is with them, so he might be able to prevent trouble, but I wouldn't be surprised if this reservation is crawling with soldiers within a month."

"I do not like the soldiers being here. I want Brenna to leave."

"It's a good idea," Kirby agreed quickly, plainly relieved. "I'll be glad to take her back to the Bar C."

Brenna shook her head. "I told him—I'm not going to leave him up here alone."

Brown grinned wryly. "I'm not alone with five hundred shuffling Miniconjou around."

Failing to see the angry sparks in her eyes, Kirby insisted, "Don't be stubborn, Brenna. Brown will rest easier if you're away from here, and so will the rest of us."

"He stays, I stay, so no more argument, please."

Kirby looked at her keenly and apparently decided he would waste his time to say anything else. "I'm going out to see this dancing for myself, before it's dark. I'll leave early in the morning."

"But first, tell me about Mendy. How's she doing as a married lady? If she argues with Ike the way she does with me, they're having a stormy time, I bet."

Kirby's face took on its familiar smile. "Oh, she and Ike still act like lovebirds. She sent you a pie of some kind, but I carried it in the saddlebags, so don't expect much."

"What about White Dove?"

"Back at the agency, teaching." His eyes searched hers tenderly. "Been really lonesome down there with all of you gone." He shook his head, trying to erase the thought, and lifted the flap of the door.

Brown threw a coat around his shoulders. "I'll go, too, and take care of your horse."

"Stay in here tonight," Brenna invited, and Kirby nodded his acceptance. She knew she'd be uncomfortable with Kirby sleeping near her and Brown. Would she ever get over her infatuation for him? No doubt in her mind, she loved Brown, but she hadn't entirely lost her penchant for Kirby.

Kirby came back before Brown did, and Brenna said quickly, "One of the reasons I won't leave is that he's about to decide to leave the reservation. I'm biding my time until both of us can leave together."

"I shouldn't have spoken up, but I'm worried about you. You're not used to living this way, and Stuart thinks it's going to be a bad winter. You could sicken and die."

"I'll be all right—" she stopped as Brown came in.

They huddled close to the fire while they ate the venison stew that Brenna had prepared and then talked of the Indians' affairs.

Later Kirby didn't show any sign of embarrassment when Brenna pointed to the pile of blankets he could use for his bedroll, so she hoped he accepted the situation without bitterness. But for once, snuggling warmly in Brown's arms didn't bring drowsiness, and she lay awake for many hours.

With a deepening foreboding, Brenna watched Kirby set out for the Bar C the next day, wishing they could have gone with him. Her fears continued to mount when Brown reported the increased presence of soldiers around the camp.

"They're keeping an eye on Big Foot for some reason. Every time I go out to check on the cattle or go to the house site, someone follows me."

About a week after Kirby left, they had just settled for the evening, when a boy bolted into the tepee.

"Sitting Bull's been killed. Big Foot says come to see him."

Brenna slumped to the ground, her stomach churning. The death of Sitting Bull just might touch off an Indian war. Knowing she couldn't stand the uncertainty of waiting until Brown returned with news, she wrapped a blanket around her shoulders and followed him out of the tepee.

14

The ground in front of Big Foot's camp crawled with excited Indians, and many of them appeared to be strangers.

"Hunkpapas," Brown murmured. "Sitting Bull's band."

Big Foot motioned Brown inside the tepee, and Brenna, not caring if she were breaking a rule of Sioux etiquette, squeezed in behind him.

Brenna gasped for breath in the odorous enclosure, but even with the fire from the smoke pit and the body heat of unwashed humans, the tepee was frigid. When Brown dropped, cross-legged, into the circle around the chief, she sat behind him and wrapped the blanket more closely around her body.

"Sitting Bull was killed, and about four hundred Hunkpapas fled the Standing Rock reservation. Most surrendered, but about a hundred came here for safety," Big Foot said as he gasped for breath. "They bring word that Colonel Sumner has orders to arrest me."

From the look of the chief, he wouldn't live long enough to be arrested.

"So that's why the soldiers have been around here," Brown commented.

"Now what do we do? I have not done anything to be arrested for. I'm not afraid, but what of my people? They'd be so afraid without me."

"Mebbe we should go talk to Colonel Sumner. His camp's not far away. I'll go, too—tell him you're peaceful," Brown said.

"Yes, that would be good," the chief said and struggled to his feet. Brenna decided that Big Foot must have wanted Brown for this purpose. Maybe he would fulfill his vision on the reservation after all.

"Saddle my horse, Brown. I'm going with you," Brenna said, and he made no protest. She rushed back to the tepee for her long cloak before she followed Brown and Big Foot out of camp. They hadn't ridden far when they encountered a cavalry detachment on patrol. Brown motioned Brenna up beside them.

"You talk," Brown said to her. He held up his hand, and the cavalrymen rode carefully toward them, hands on their guns.

"Will you take us to Colonel Sumner, please?" Brenna said to the captain.

The amazement on the man's face brought a smile to her lips. "A white woman!" he gulped.

"Yes, late of Philadelphia, but right now a member of Big Foot's band of Miniconjou. Big Foot," she motioned to the chief, "wants to see Colonel Sumner to find out why the cavalry has his camp under surveillance."

Too stunned for words, the captain ordered his men about face and motioned for the three riders to follow him. A few cavalrymen brought up the rear.

"Good," Brown approved quietly. "Maybe you're the White Buffalo Calf Maiden after all."

A half-hour ride brought them to a tent encampment not

far from the Cheyenne River agent's headquarters. Colonel Sumner received them without surprise. Again Brown motioned for Brenna to speak.

"This is my husband, Brown Bear; we're living with Big Foot's band. The chief and his people are alarmed by the many soldiers on the reservation. Today, a group of Hunkpapas arrived, saying that Sitting Bull has been killed. The chief would like to know why the army of the Great Father has turned against the Sioux."

"The army had nothing to do with Sitting Bull's death," Colonel Sumner commented testily. "Better ask the Sioux about that, but as for my presence here, a few weeks ago the Indian bureau in Washington asked the agents to send names of those who were responsible for this ghost dancing. The names of Sitting Bull and Big Foot headed that list. I received orders several days ago from General Miles in Chicago to arrest Big Foot, but I've delayed—not sure it was a good idea."

Brown held up his hand and said, "The Sioux have done nothing to deserve arrest. Does not the white man practice his religion? Does not the Sioux have that right? The ghost dancing will stop before the winter ends, for the Sioux are starving. To arrest Big Foot is a mistake."

"I know that. You know that. But the big brass in Washington don't know it, and I have to take orders."

"Bad orders," Brown insisted.

"I've decided to act anyway," Sumner said. "I'm not going to arrest Big Foot, but I want him to take his whole band into the Pine Ridge Agency, where we can keep our eye on them." He turned to Big Foot. "Order your people to move there immediately."

"I do not mind going to the agency, but there may be trouble with my people. Many women and children are too cold and hungry to leave village."

"They're not too cold and hungry to dance, I've observed."

The colonel turned to Brown and Brenna. "You have a few days to convince him to move his people to Pine Ridge. Any suspicious actions, and I'll bring in the troops."

He signaled that the interview was over, and Brenna held out her hand, displaying all the charm she could muster. "Thank you very much."

"I must say I'm curious, ma'am, about your presence here."

"It's a long story, colonel. Maybe another time."

Back in his tepee, the chief made his report, adding, "It may be well for us to move to the agency. No food here."

The younger men wildly opposed his suggestion, and the medicine man, Yellow Hand, objected, "No, keep dancing. Put on shirts and dance. Let pony soldiers shoot, won't hurt us."

"I think we should move to Pine Ridge," Brown counseled.

Yellow Hand resented his comment, and Brown said no more. After all, Big Foot would make the decision. Slowly the ailing chief said, "Wait and see—don't want to happen to me what happened to Sitting Bull."

Brown motioned for Brenna to follow him away from the council. "Go on to the tepee, and I'll come soon as I find out what did happen to Sitting Bull." After questioning several of the Hunkpapa refugees, Brown brought Brenna the sad tale of the death of one of the great Sioux chiefs, and she recorded it in her notebook as he talked.

McLaughlin, the agent at Standing Rock, had never liked Sitting Bull, and he blamed the chief for the ghost-dance trouble, considering it a trick so that Sitting Bull could establish himself as the sole Sioux leader. When the agent learned that Sitting Bull planned to visit the Pine Ridge Agency, he decided to arrest the old chief before he could leave.

Knowing that Sitting Bull's followers would be outraged at the act, McLaughlin assigned the task to Indian policemen led by Bull Head. One night about forty Sioux police converged on Sitting Bull's Grand River camp, and at dawn they surrounded the chief's cabin. A squadron of cavalry waited a few miles away, ready to intervene if trouble erupted.

When the police dragged Sitting Bull from his bed to arrest him, he offered no protest, but when Bull Head emerged from the cabin with his prisoner, a crowd of ghost dancers had gathered outside. Intent on preventing the arrest, one of the dancers fired a shot, and in the ensuing melee, Sitting Bull was killed.

Brown smiled sadly when he concluded, "During the gunfire, the old show horse that Buffalo Bill gave Sitting Bull started doing his tricks. He sat up, lifted one hoof, and scared everybody. They thought he did the ghost dance, too."

Tears filled Brenna's eyes, and Brown pulled her close. "Don't weep for Sitting Bull. He's better off dead, not having to see the end of Sioux."

"His prophecy came true, after all. Remember when he visited the Bar C, he said he'd had a vision that he'd be killed by his own people."

A few days passed without Colonel Sumner making a move, and Big Foot's band continued their dancing. Brenna began to hope that trouble would be avoided after all, until Brown became concerned about the unusual activity in the camp.

"They're excited about something, and I don't like it." Late that day, when he learned the Miniconjou planned to escape from Colonel Sumner's watching eye, he groaned, "Worst thing they can do. I feel sure they'll go to join Short Bull in the Badlands."

He went to Big Foot to try to persuade the old man to cooperate with the army. "If you move, better go to Pine Ridge, the way Colonel Sumner told you." But when Big Foot remained noncommittal about his destination, Brown came to a rapid decision.

"I'll leave Big Foot's band today. I'll take my Brenna away—going to be war, and I don't want her in it."

A fierce look came over the old man's face. *"Piedra de toque* stays with us. The White Buffalo Calf Maiden does not leave the Sioux. Prepare to go with us at nightfall."

"He can have his old *piedra de toque*," Brenna said, when Brown told her what the chief had said. "I wish I'd never opened that trunk of Dad's. If you want to leave here, let's go. I'm frightened."

"Help me make ready." Brown put a framework of poles over their wagon and wrapped a canvas over the frame. They packed all their belongings into the wagon, leaving enough space for them to sleep.

"Bad weather will come, and it takes several days to arrive at Bar C. Have to have shelter."

Although they'd hurried, they weren't ready to leave until late afternoon. Brown had kept an apprehensive eye on the Indian camp all afternoon, and when he started to pull across the creek, a score or more of mounted, armed Indians, led by Yellow Hand, surrounded the wagon.

"Go with Big Foot," Yellow Bird intoned ominously.

Brown slumped in defeat and threw an apologetic glance toward Brenna. Without her, he'd probably have defied the Indians, but she knew he wouldn't take risks with her on the wagon seat. As they turned back toward Big Foot's camp, Brenna experienced the most hopeless feeling she'd ever known, and Brown must have sensed her trauma, because he took her hand.

"Don't worry. I'll take you away somehow."

For his sake, she tried to overcome her panic. "As long as I'm with you, I'll be all right."

But before that night ended, Brenna started to wonder if both of them were doomed to perish. There must have been over three hundred people with Big Foot, and how the chief thought he could sneak away under the eyes of the United

States Army, she couldn't imagine. By daylight the cavalry still hadn't overtaken them, and to take her mind off the danger they faced, Brenna wrote in her notebook. If she survived this predicament, she'd have all she needed for a book about the Sioux.

Lack of rest and the shaking wagon, made her writing little more than a scrawl, but at least she had something to do besides looking over her shoulder to see if Colonel Sumner's men had caught up with them.

December 27, 1890

Writing this date gave me a shock, for I can't believe that Christmas Day passed without any notice. Hard to believe, too, that I'm practically a prisoner, bouncing along this rocky ground, surrounded by three hundred freezing, starving, miserable Sioux, who are running away from the United States Cavalry. To think that last Christmas I was safe in Philadelphia, concerned only with trimming the tree and helping Mendy bake cookies for the orphanage down the street.

As I look at these wretched remnants of humanity around me, I can't imagine why our government thinks they pose a threat to anyone. I suffer shame for my people. But who are my people? Looking at the worried face of my dear husband, I feel at one with him, and Sioux blood is prevalent in my veins. But when my body complains about the cold and discomfort I'm suffering, then I realize my white heritage prevails.

She laid her notebook aside and crowded close to Brown, eager for his warmth.

Even his compassionate look warmed her. "Lie down in the wagon. It will rest you. Be warmer."

"I'm happier close to you. When do you think he'll stop? These people look ready to drop now."

All day Big Foot kept his flock moving, even though the

old chief himself had taken sick and lay in a jolting wagon. When they stopped for the night, in spite of her irritation that the chief had insisted that they accompany his people, Brenna went to inquire about him.

"Sick," he whispered, and she shuddered at his deplorable condition. His blankets were spotted with blood, and bloody specks clung to his face. He struggled for each breath, and she wondered if he didn't have pneumonia in addition to the tuberculosis. She'd be surprised if he lived through the night.

"What will happen if Big Foot dies?" Brenna asked Brown when they sought the privacy of their wagon.

"Hard to tell—old chief keeps us together," Brown answered glumly.

Not knowing how long their meager supplies would have to last, Brown and Brenna ate sparingly, and for the first time in her life, Brenna went to bed hungry. But hunger didn't dull their desire for each other, and while they clung together, the outside world and its dangers held no fear for them.

"Do you want to know a secret?" Brenna whispered, while Brown moved his lips across hers.

"Mebbe. Don't always like secrets."

"You'll like this one—you're going to be a papa."

His arms tightened, and she heard the quick intake of his breath.

"Sure?"

"Yes. Probably about the Moon When Ponies Shed."

"Why didn't you tell me before?"

"I didn't want my condition to interfere with your decision to leave the reservation. Now that you've decided to go, I thought you should know."

"You like the idea?"

"Of course. I love you, and bearing your child is the reward we have for love. You like the idea?" she whispered.

He answered by once again pulling her close, and the camp was awakening around them when they next stirred.

By mid-afternoon the cavalry caught up with Big Foot's band. Brenna had hoped that Colonel Sumner's troops would be their captors, but when Big Foot raised a white flag on his wagon, the stranger who came forward introduced himself as Major Samuel Whitside.

Checking the markings on the equipment, Brown muttered, "Custer's old troops—no good for us."

Whitside announced in a steady voice, "I have orders to take you with us to our camp on Wounded Knee Creek."

Big Foot nodded. "Going that way to Pine Ridge. Needed protection for our people."

"We'll protect you," the major said. "Disarm them."

A half-breed scout riding beside him argued, "Not a good idea, Major. These men are hostile, and if we try to disarm them, there'll be a fight. Lots of women and kids here will be killed."

The major acquiesced ungraciously, but he did order an ambulance for Big Foot, saying it would be an easier ride for the sick man. Once the chief was transferred, Whitside formed a column for the march. Half the cavalry took the lead, while two other troops fell in behind the Indians. Uneasily Brown eyed the numerous Springfield rifles and the two Hotchkiss guns rattling along at the rear of the procession, and he approached Major Whitside.

"Major, my wife is a white woman, and we've been living with Big Foot's band, but we had no part in this ghost dancing. Will you give permission for me to take her south to my stepbrother at the Bar-C ranch?"

Obviously the Bar-C ranch was known to the major, for he took a closer look at Brenna.

"A white woman?" he said.

"Yes," Brenna replied. "Brown Bear and I were married last autumn. He had lived at the Bar C for years but moved to the reservation hoping he could help his people. He tried to counsel them to avoid this ghost dancing, but they wouldn't listen. I'm expecting a child, and we made plans a few days ago to return to the Bar C."

"Then what are you doing with Big Foot's people?"

"We started south when we learned they were leaving the Cheyenne agency, but we were forced to come along on this march."

Looking at the sky, Whitside said wearily, "I hate making war on women and children. It will be dark soon, so stay with us tonight, and I'll let you leave tomorrow as soon as we reach Pine Ridge. You're safe enough with us." His answer reassured Brenna, but she looked often at Brown, whose face grew more solemn as they continued the journey. Little daylight remained when the mass of people descended the slope into Wounded Knee Creek.

While the Sioux set up camp, Whitside had a stove placed in Big Foot's tepee and asked one of his surgeons to check the chief. The major also provided tents to the Sioux without shelter, and the soldiers handed out rations to the hungry Indians.

Brown politely refused the rations and the tent, saying, "We sleep in our wagon, and we have food."

Because of the intense cold, made worse by a northeast wind, they decided to eat in the wagon, but Brown did use some of the firewood he'd slung under the wagon to brew a pot of coffee. He passed two tins of the warm liquid into the wagon and took what was left in the pot to the Indians camped close to them before he joined Brenna in the wagon.

"Whitside has been pretty decent, I'd say," Brenna commented.

"Yes, but he'll make sure no one escapes. The Sioux are surrounded with troops, and he placed two big cannon on top of the hill above the camp. Wouldn't take long for those guns to kill everybody."

"So he's ready for trouble."

"And one wrong move is all it takes to start it. How I wish I'd taken you away from here long ago."

As soon as they ate some cold bread and dried venison, they rolled into their blankets, and Brown's nearness brought Brenna a sense of well-being. Feeling the tenseness of his body, she knew that Brown would probably lie awake all night.

"If it weren't for me, would you leave the Sioux? Am I the only reason you're going away?"

"Probably. But I told you long ago—I've been at war inside. I like the white man's ways, but it bothers me to feel as if I deserted my people, so I'm not content at Bar C. Then I came to the Sioux, following my vision, but I don't fit here either."

When a man loses his dreams, what does he have left?

"When we leave tomorrow, should we give the touchstone to Big Foot?"

"I do not care. I know now there's no power in the *piedra de toque*—just a pretty ornament. If there were power in it, your coming would have helped the Sioux more. I should not have demanded it of you, but I had to try. Had to do what I could for my people."

Brenna quivered at the hopelessness in his voice. Could she help him restore hope within? Was her love enough to bring him happiness? Surely when their child was born, he'd be more satisfied in the white man's world.

"The Indian is dead, Brenna, but give us credit, it took a long time to destroy us."

"I suppose the destruction of Indian culture has been inevitable since the first wagon train crossed the Mississippi River."

"Long before that! When Europeans first stepped on this continent, they sounded the death knell for the Indian, but it took almost four hundred years to finish us off. We don't die easily—we take a long time to die."

All this talk of death bothered Brenna. "Many Sioux remain, in spite of all their trouble. There has to be some future for them."

"Someday the Sioux may be strong again, but I'll not live to see it." He placed his hand on her stomach. "My son, mebbe, but not me. Teach him the best of both worlds."

"Of course, it may not be a son!" Brenna said lightly, hoping to stir him from the somber mood.

"It'll be a son!" he said as if he had no doubt about it.

He turned to her and seemed to relax as he caressed her body with his hands and lips. For the moment they forgot the miserable Sioux outside their wagon, forgot the army surrounding them, forgot the danger and hardship that might wait for them tomorrow, forgot everything but their love and need for each other.

"Whatever happens," Brenna whispered, "I want you to know that I've never been sorry I married you. The love we've shared has been the greatest experience of my life."

"Yes," he answered. "Only with you have I found contentment, only with you have I felt a whole person. I have great love for you. And I want you to know, I have renounced the religion of my fathers. I have remembered my decision at Carlisle years ago. I claim a verse I learned there as my hope, 'Peace I leave with you, my peace I give unto you: not as the world giveth, give I unto you. Let not your heart be troubled, neither let it be afraid.' My dear Brenna, the battle is over at last, and neither the white man nor Indian won. The Christ has given me peace within."

"Brown, I love you. Whatever the future holds, we'll face it together."

Although Brenna thought she couldn't, she did sleep fitfully, but each time she stirred, she sensed that Brown tensely watched out the night. Was he worried about what the soldiers or the Indians might do?

Up at first light, Brown vacated the wagon, but soon he reported back to her. "More soldiers arrived during the night—two more big guns on the hill. Whitside's not in charge now, man by the name of Forsyth—a lot more soldiers now than Sioux, but Little Bat's with the soldiers; mebbe he can keep trouble away."

They'd only eaten a few bites of food when soldiers swarmed through the Sioux encampment, calling, "All men gather at Big Foot's tepee."

"I'll go, but you stay here a bit."

Brenna raised the curtain beside the driver's seat so she could at least see what was going on. Bright Star came and crawled into the wagon with her. Little Bat passed the wagon. With a startled look on his face, he tipped his hat, and said, "Miss, you ought not to be here."

The male Indians came out of their tepees, wearing ghost shirts, and sat in a semicircle around Big Foot, who had been carried from his tepee and placed on the ground. Soldiers, with guns aimed and ready, surrounded the Indians.

"All of you are to turn in your arms," Forsyth announced, "and prepare to march to Pine Ridge Agency. Consider yourselves our prisoners."

The soldiers herded the Indians twenty at a time to the tepees, demanding their guns. Brown came back to their wagon and took his rifle to the soldiers. At the end of the search, only one other rifle had been collected.

Colonel Forsyth's face turned an angry red. "Search their tepees. Take everything they've hidden."

The soldiers pulled the Indians' possessions out of their tepees, ripped open their bags, and strewed the contents out on the ground. If a woman protested the confiscation of the knife she used in food preparation, the soldiers shoved her aside. A few tents folded up on the scuffling cavalrymen and the Sioux women.

"Going to be bad trouble," Bright Star said.

While the search continued, Yellow Bird started the steps of the ghost dance. "Don't pay attention to them, do not give up your arms. The bullets will not pierce your sacred shirts. Do not fear."

When the medicine man voiced his protest, Brown moved quickly to their wagon, and Brenna stepped down to stand beside him. Tension thickened the air until Brenna felt stifled. When the soldiers started to ransack their wagon, Little Bat said a few quick words to Forsyth, and the colonel waved the soldiers aside. At that moment, Brenna felt the surge of her Sioux blood and didn't even care that they'd spared her. The Sioux may have had their rebellious days, but here Brenna could see nothing but hungry, harried women and children.

When that search netted only a small collection of knives and old guns, Forsyth commanded the soldiers to search the Indians themselves. What happened then occurred too fast for Brenna to comprehend.

The soldiers approached one young Miniconjou, and he backed away, holding a new Winchester menacingly. Two cavalrymen grabbed him, spun him around, and took hold of the gun. In the scramble, the gun fired, and a soldier fell. The other soldiers answered with a point-blank volley, and more than half the Sioux warriors around Big Foot's tepee struck the ground. Brenna saw Big Foot collapse when a bullet pierced him, and she screamed when she felt her body falling, until she realized Brown had pushed her to the ground.

"Lie still," he commanded, and he covered her body with his as the Hotchkiss guns on the hills sent a volley of shells into the camp.

Bright Star ran from their wagon, and her body fell in front of Brenna's eyes, a bullet wound in her head. Shells thudded into bodies. Women and children screamed. Brenna peered cautiously from the protection of Brown's body, to see men, women, and children trying to escape, only to fall when bullets struck them. A few warriors fought the soldiers at close quarters with clubs, pistols, and knives. Powder smoke was so thick that Brenna choked.

Yellow Bird still stood, and he spread wide his arms. "The sacred shirt protects me," he shouted and then crumbled into a heap. A shell struck nearby, and Brenna felt Brown's body jerk.

She screamed again. "Did they hit you?"

"Lie still," he whispered. "No matter about me—want to save you and the boy."

Tears flowed from her eyes, and she tried to reach a hand to him, but his body was a dead weight. Blood from his wound moistened her side. Suddenly the area seemed quiet, deserted, and she saw dozens of women and children running toward a little ravine, trying to escape the raking fire, but one of the Hotchkiss guns changed its position and swept the ravine with fire, cutting down anything that moved.

Brown's body went slack over hers, and she moaned. He couldn't be dead; maybe he'd only fainted. The battle had moved from the camp now, and though she feared moving, she had to tend to Brown's wound. She wriggled out from under his limp body and sat up, shivering, as blowing snow struck her garments wet with Brown's blood. She gagged when she saw his mutilated back and the blood that soaked his clothing.

"Brown," she cried, trying to lift his head. She felt for a pulse, but could feel no sign of life. Sensing a movement beside her, she looked up at two soldiers who walked nearby. One of them spit on Bright Star's body, and said, "Guess that avenges Custer."

Brenna retched, and the soldier swung toward her, his gun raised.

"Kill her," his companion said. "She's seen too much."

She jumped to her feet angrily, her sickness forgotten. "Oh, so you'll kill me to still my tongue, will you? You've killed my husband, so kill me, too, but you'll never be free from this moment. What you've done here today will follow you to the end of your lives."

"A white woman!" one of them said.

"No, I'm Sioux. Sioux, do you hear?" She pulled the touchstone from her dress and waved it in their faces. "I'm the White Buffalo Calf Maiden, and I'll haunt you forever."

The cavalryman collapsed at her feet, and she looked at the touchstone with something akin to awe, until she noticed that the dying Yellow Hand had lifted his gun and shot the soldier. The other cavalryman, started for a moment, raised his gun, but he was diverted by the sound of two horses racing down the slope and into the water of the creek.

Kirby and Stuart!

Brenna ran toward them, shouting, "Help me, he's going to kill me."

Both men jumped from their saddles, and Kirby shoved Brenna behind him while Stuart lifted a gun and halted the advancing soldier.

"What's happened here?" Kirby said, surveying the scene of slaughter.

"It's been a nightmare, and I think they've killed Brown. Come, help me."

While Stuart and Kirby attempted to revive Brown, Brenna poured out the bitter story of the past week. "None of them had a chance," she sobbed bitterly.

"When I returned to the Bar C, and told Stuart what was going on, he'd learned that the soldiers had been ordered to the reservation. We were afraid you and Brown would be in trouble, so we rushed up here. If we'd been a few minutes later, it would have been too late."

"It *is* too late for him," Brenna cried. "If only you'd come a few minutes sooner, to have saved Brown. I don't want to live without him. I wish I'd died, too."

She threw her arms around Brown, sobbing, knowing she'd never again hear his voice and share his love.

Kirby's voice broke when he tried to speak, but he finally said, "He was my brother—let's take him home to the Bar C for burial."

Little Bat had come back while they worked over Brown, and he spoke to Stuart. "I'd get her away from here if I were you—these soldiers are bloodthirsty."

"Yes, Kirby, let's move—we can't afford to have a fight with the army."

Brenna staggered to her feet and looked around the little valley littered with hundreds of bodies. She saw several dead soldiers, most of whom had been killed by their own comrades, for the Sioux hadn't possessed the weapons to inflict such wounds. Wind whipped snow across the creek bottom, and Stuart rummaged in the wagon and came out with Brenna's coat, which did little to cut the sting of the wind.

Rifle fire sounded sporadically in the ravine where the Indians had fled. The soldiers nearby, demoralized by the death they'd perpetrated, paid no heed to them, and Kirby and Stuart carefully wrapped Brown's body in a blanket and laid him in the wagon. Brenna settled down beside his body while Stuart hitched the team and drove the wagon out of the creek bottom. Kirby followed behind, leading the extra horses.

Brenna caressed Brown's face and tried not to think, but it was impossible to drown the memory of Brown's voice from the night before. "The Indian is dead . . . but give us credit, we don't die easily."

15

Not even the day her parents died had Brenna experienced such a sense of despair. Reeling back and forth as the wagon jolted along the uneven, frozen ground, she endured the discomfort, wanting as much as Stuart to put Wounded Knee Creek and its memories behind her. When the wagon careened, she put out a protective hand to steady Brown's body, often forgetting that it made no difference to him now.

The cold intensified, and Brenna took one of the blankets they'd put over Brown and draped it around her shoulders. She had to keep telling herself that he didn't need any warmth now, but his child did. She rubbed her hands along the wool blanket, remembering how he had held her under this covering last night. As she relived those caresses she'd never know again, the tears cascaded from her eyes.

They rode for about three hours before Stuart stopped the horses, and he and Kirby climbed inside the wagon. The wind had reddened their faces, and icicles hung from their hair.

Rubbing his hands together, Stuart said, "I thought for a

while that I was going blind, until it dawned on me that ice was freezing over my eyes. What are we going to do, Kirby? We can't camp out in this weather."

"The closest shelter is at Pine Ridge. How far are we from there?"

"About ten miles, I'd judge, and I think we can make it before dark, if the horses hold out. Brenna, is there anything to eat in here?"

Glad to have something to occupy her hands, she pulled a basket from under the driver's seat. "We'd loaded up everything we had, and were planning to head south, but the Indians wouldn't let us leave them. When we met up with the cavalry, Brown asked Major Whitside for permission to leave, and he agreed we could go today." She bit her lips to stop trembling. "Just one day too late."

Stuart took the basket from her and changed the subject rapidly. "You have some canned food, which will do fine. Provide us food and liquid, too. This will last until we get home, even if we can't pick up anything at Pine Ridge." He opened a can of peaches with his knife, handed it to Brenna, and found two more for himself and Kirby.

"We're in for a blizzard," Kirby said, "so we'll be stuck at Pine Ridge a few days if we do stop. But even there, Brenna can't stay in this wagon. Wonder what kind of shelter we can find?"

"How about Dove's little schoolhouse?" Brenna said. "There's a couple of cots and a stove in the room back of the classroom."

"That's the place!" Stuart exclaimed. "She closed the school about mid-December because most of her pupils had gone ghost dancing. She's at the Bar C, so we can hole up there, if somebody else hasn't already had the same idea. These hills are full of soldiers who are going to look for shelter."

"Let's hope the horses hold out," Kirby said as he left the

wagon. The afternoon waned and the wind grew stronger, whipping the canvas, until the interior of the wagon was covered with fine snow.

"At last," Brenna heard Stuart say with a note of relief in his voice. She peered through the canvas opening.

"Are we at Pine Ridge?"

"Yes, and none too soon for the horses—or for me, for that matter." Brenna moved out to sit beside him on the seat as he skirted the agency buildings and pulled up in front of the deserted schoolhouse. The door was locked, but in spite of the fact that his hands were stiff with cold, Kirby used a knife to gain entrance and turned to lift Brenna off the wagon seat.

"What about him?" Brenna asked, motioning inside the wagon. She knew it was foolish, but she couldn't enjoy shelter if Brown's body had to remain out in the elements.

"There's an outbuilding here where we can stable the horses and enclose the wagon. It'll be crowded, but at least they'll be out of the snow and wind."

She shuddered when she thought that if Stuart and Kirby hadn't come when they did, both she and Brown would be lying out in the blizzard.

Kirby started a fire in the stove in Dove's living quarters as well as in the schoolroom. "Glad there's a supply of wood laid in," he commented.

Brenna checked through Dove's food supply, and finding some coffee beans, she asked Kirby to bring water from the barrel outside the building while she started grinding the coffee. "Maybe you'd better bring in the rest of the food from the wagon. Dove didn't leave much except some dried apples and beans, which will take too long to prepare tonight."

After they'd eaten some canned tomatoes and jerky, Stuart went over to the agency, and when he returned, covered with snow, and shivering from the cold, his face was stony with anger.

"What took you so long?" Kirby asked.

"The wagons are coming in with survivors, and I helped unload them. Twenty-five soldiers are dead and almost forty wounded."

"Then they must have shot their own men," Brenna said, "because they'd taken most of the Sioux' weapons."

"They've also brought in the wounded Sioux—four men and forty-seven women and children. They're lying out in the cold while the soldiers look for shelter. I think they've decided to house them at the Episcopal mission."

"Be kinda crowded, won't it?" Kirby said.

"They took the benches out and scattered hay on the floor."

"Fifty survivors!" Brenna cried, "and there were over three hundred of us when we left Big Foot's camp. It's nothing but murder. No one had anything to fear from the Sioux."

"Most of the old chiefs are gone now," Stuart said, "so it's all downhill for those who are left."

Brenna placed her hand on her stomach and thought of the Sioux child forming within her. What kind of future could she make for him?

Kirby and Stuart rolled into blankets in the schoolroom, leaving Brenna the small room.

"I'll come in a few times and put wood on the fire," Stuart told her, "so don't be disturbed. I'll try not to wake you."

She hadn't even been to sleep when Stuart came in the first time, for her thoughts were too tumultuous. After she'd taken Brown to the ranch for burial, then what? It was impossible for her to stay at the Bar C now.

Brenna fingered the touchstone. It had brought her much trouble, though without it, she was sure Brown would never have married her. Not even to have avoided the sorrow she knew tonight would she have denied herself those six months with him.

Never one to vacillate long over a decision, by morning

Brenna knew she would burn her bridges behind her, since she could never return anyway.

The blizzard continued for two more days. Brenna cooked a large pot of beans, stewed some tinned tomatoes, and made the apples into a cobbler, so they had enough to eat. That took her most of the first day, but she wanted to stay busy. Stuart made some creditable biscuits the second day, and they managed well enough. The two men stayed close to the building, leaving only to look after the horses.

For hours Stuart sprawled on the floor near the stove and read the few volumes that Dove had on the bookshelf.

"Been a long time since I'd read *Robin Hood*," he said.

Kirby prowled around the room aimlessly, staring out the windows at the drifting snow.

"There's not a thing we can do till the storm stops, Kirby, so sit down and take it easy," Stuart advised.

Once her decision had been made, Brenna sat quietly. On the second day she said, "I think I should tell you what my plans are."

Kirby came quickly to her side. "You're welcome to remain at the Bar C. In fact, I *want* you to stay there."

She shook her head. "No, I won't stay, although that might be the easiest way. I'm going back to Philadelphia."

"Brenna!" Kirby pleaded.

"I figgered you'd do that," Stuart said, "and maybe it's for the best."

"Well, thanks a lot, Stuart," Kirby said bitterly and turned to stare out the window again. Brenna could sense his disappointment. *Why must I always blight his hopes?*

"I need to return for business reasons, if nothing else," she continued. "I have the Andersons' house and other affairs to take care of. When I left, I had no idea of being out here so long."

"That's a long trip alone," Stuart said. "One of us should take you."

"Mendy will jump at the chance to go back home, and if I keep that big house, Ike would be useful, too."

"Does that mean you'll never return?" Kirby asked.

"I don't know. I need some time to decide what I will do. Eighteen-ninety has been a trying time for me," she said wearily. "In less than a year I've lost my adopted parents, found my real father, married, and become a widow. Before I make any major decisions about the future, I have to accept what has happened to me. I haven't done that yet."

"It just makes sense, Kirby," Stuart said. "Can't you see that?"

Kirby didn't answer, and Brenna continued, "I intend to write that book about the Sioux."

By New Year's Day, the storm passed, but before they left for the Bar C, Stuart and Kirby rode out to Wounded Knee with some soldiers and other civilians. From the bleak expressions on their faces when they returned, Brenna knew the experience had been a bad one.

"I might as well know the worst of it," she said.

"Frozen bodies were scattered all over the valley," Stuart said. "The soldiers dug a big pit, dragged bodies from the snow, and dumped them all in together. They found four babies that were still alive, but no other survivors. The soldiers looted the bodies, even took some of those crazy ghost shirts. It was enough to make anybody sick, so we finally left."

"We're heading out of here in the morning," Kirby said, "and it's going to be cold, so bundle up."

"In the meantime," Stuart said, "somebody had better be thinking of the way to break this news to Dove and Tatoke."

Brenna went to the two men, hovering over the stove, and put her arms around them. "If you hadn't come when you did, Brown and I would have been out there, too. I don't believe I've even thanked you, but you've always been there when I needed you. At first, I wished I could have died when he did, but now that I've had time to think about it, I know the best thing I can do for Brown is to live—you see, I'm carrying his child."

Brenna felt Kirby's body tense beside her, and he didn't reply.

"When?" Stuart asked.

"July."

Without trouble they arrived at the Bar C and made arrangements for Brown's immediate burial. The cowhands dug a grave while Stuart built the coffin. With Tatoke and Dove beside her, Brenna looked at Brown for the last time. She draped the touchstone carefully on Brown's chest. The hopes of the Sioux were dead, so the *piedra de toque* might as well be buried, too. She'd decided this was the way to get rid of the troublesome necklace once and for all.

The chaplain from Fort Robinson, who'd married them, came to preside at the simple burial service, and before he left, he handed Brenna a wrapped package.

"Here are the pictures of your wedding day," he said kindly, apparently having forgiven her for marrying an Indian. "I'm sorry they couldn't have been presented at a happier time."

Back in the ranch house, she unwrapped the brown paper, and when she saw their happy faces and remembered all the pleasures they'd enjoyed during their marriage, the tears she couldn't shed at the gravesite began to fall. At least, she thought, she would have these pictures to show his son.

As she'd predicted, as soon as Mendy heard that Brenna planned to return to Philadelphia, she announced, "Ike and me, we're goin' with you."

Brenna didn't even argue. "Thank you, Mendy, I'll appreciate it."

On the night before she left the ranch, Kirby asked to see her alone. "I want you to know," he said, "that I didn't wish him to die. It's haunted me that I might have wanted him out of the way and that you might think I wished he were dead."

Aghast, Brenna stared at Kirby. "I never thought of such a thing. Right from the first, you didn't seem to be bitter about us."

"Not bitter, but I hurt more than I showed. I still want you, Brenna. Perhaps it isn't the time to say so, but I had to speak before you left here. I want to marry you, want to help you bring up your child."

"My child will be aware of his Sioux heritage, and I want him to respect his father. I've made up my mind to that."

"That's the way it should be, but can you do that alone? I understand Sioux ways, have respect for them, and I can help you. But I won't pressure you now. Go back to Philadelphia, but I believe that once you're over the grief of his death, you'll know it's right for you to live here."

Brenna nodded. "I'm not running away, but I don't want to make a hasty decision. I loved both of you, but it seemed right to go with Brown. Now I know why. I made him happy, and if he'd been killed without having me with him, I'd never have forgiven myself."

She wiped away her tears, and Kirby said, "Don't talk about it. I didn't mean to make you cry."

"No, I want to say it. He made me promise that if anything happened to him, I'd come back to the Bar C, and he told me more than once you'd make a good husband, so if we decide to marry, I wouldn't consider myself unfaithful to him. But it will take time."

Kirby's face brightened, and he replied, "I can wait."

Brenna hoped she hadn't given him any false assurance, for she felt so empty inside. Would she ever have the capacity to love anyone again? The very thought of sharing intimacy with any man, even Kirby, repulsed her.

*   *   *

While Brenna waited for the birth of her child, she worked on the manuscript. She borrowed books from the college where her father had taught. Remembering Brown's words, she entitled the book *A Long Time to Die*; she started the manuscript with the arrival of Columbus and ended it with the Battle of Wounded Knee.

Several publishers rejected the book, saying the Battle of Wounded Knee was still too controversial to have her eye-witness account appear on the bookshelves. But the first of June, a New York publisher issued a contract for the book, promising to release it early in 1892.

The last month of waiting was the hardest, and Brenna spent many hours searching the Bible for a key to her past and future. She read over and over the words from 1 Peter, "But the God of all grace, who hath called us unto his eternal glory by Christ Jesus, after that ye have suffered a while, make you perfect, stablish, strengthen, settle you."

Mendy kept her company, hovered over her, anticipating her every wish. Brenna had written several times to the Bar C, not exclusively to Kirby, but to Dove and Stuart as well, asking that they share her letters. A few days before her due date, she received a telegram, "With love from all of us at the Bar C."

She felt their presence with her when the first pangs of childbirth seared her body and through the intense agony she endured, until finally she heard the cry of her firstborn. Then Mendy's voice, said, "We got us a boy, missy. A nice little red baby."

Brenna lifted her head and looked at the child. "Thank God," she whispered. The boy looked all Indian, as if he had no white blood at all. That's the way she wanted it.

"What we gonna call him, Miss Brenna?"

"Little Brown Bear, of course," and she drifted off to sleep.

*   *   *

Brenna laid aside the advance copy of *A Long Time to Die*, and lifted Little Bear from his cradle. She rocked the active six-month-old child and rested her chin on his black hair while he nursed. What more could she do for Brown? She'd borne his child and had written a book to glorify his people.

When the baby slept again, she laid him in his cradle, covering him carefully for the night. Before dimming the light, she looked once more at her book's dedication page:

"In Memory of My Beloved Husband, Brown Bear, and of my father, John Anderson, who stirred my interest in the Sioux nation."

She'd fulfilled her duty to her father, and she could think of nothing more to do for Brown except to rear his child. She recalled Brown had said, "Teach him the best of both worlds." Could she do that in Philadelphia? If Brown could make the choice, he'd say, "Take the boy to Bar C"; she had no doubt about that. But how could she possibly go to Kirby when her need for Brown hadn't abated at all?

The time had come to let him go, but how could she? While she wrestled with her decision, she lived again every word he'd said to her, every moment they'd shared: The first day he'd kissed her on the way home from Crawford. The time they'd gone to *Wakantepee* and he'd told her about his childhood vision. The agony he'd endured at the sun dance. The day she'd revealed her possession of the touchstone, and he'd taken her to be the White Buffalo Calf Maiden. Their wedding day and the honeymoon trip to Big Foot's camp. The hopes they'd shared, and last of all, she remembered his death at Wounded Knee, how he'd protected her with his own body.

She wanted to live with his memory, yet she knew the time had come to let him go in peace. He had died as a Christian, so what more could she ask? Brenna accepted his death at last, but with that release, she erupted into wild sobbing that brought Mendy hustling to her bedside.

Mendy gathered her into warm arms that had been a childhood refuge, and she comforted her as if Brenna were still a child. "Poor missy, cry it out on Mendy's shoulder till the hurt goes away."

When the storm of agony finally passed, Brenna whispered, "I loved him so much but I have to give him up."

"Yes, child. He wouldn't want you to be unhappy. Don't you think it's about time to go back to Mistah Kirby? Philadelphia ain't no place for a little Sioux boy. Ike and I, we'll go with you."

So again she burned her bridges behind her, and the next morning she wrote a brief letter.

Dear Kirby,

If you still want me, I'm ready to become your wife. Mendy and Ike are as eager to return to the Bar C as I am. We can start west as soon as I conclude the sale of this house.

The words sounded stilted and cold, but how could she put on paper that she loved him? She'd have to show him that, and at last, she looked forward to the opportunity.

Three weeks passed without any word from Kirby, and Brenna started to fret. Surely he could have written, telegraphed, or something by now. Had he changed his mind? She pondered this while she sat in the parlor and rocked Little Bear to sleep.

A knock sounded at the door, and knowing Mendy had gone shopping, Brenna walked quietly to the door, carrying the sleeping child in her arms. Just as she'd seen him almost five years ago when he came to their house, Kirby stood there again. Had he changed at all? His crisp russet hair waved back from his forehead, steel-blue eyes gleamed from his deeply tanned face, and the friendly smile warmed her heart. She noticed, however, some deep lines of suffering around his eyes that hadn't been there the first time. She'd helped put those lines there, and now she would try to erase them.

For a moment neither spoke, until she invited him into the parlor. "I came after you," he said. "We can be married here, and I'll take you home."

Tears brimmed in her eyes, but he wiped them away. "No more tears." He took her in his arms and kissed her, and the pressure of his embrace startled and awakened Little Bear, who set up a howl.

Kirby peered closely at the child, and looking pleased, he said, "He's Sioux all right. Doesn't look anything like you."

"That's the way I wanted it."

Reaching into his pocket, Kirby pulled out a package. As he unwrapped it, Brenna watched breathlessly. He twirled the touchstone in front of Little Bear's face.

"Where'd you get it?" she gasped.

"I thought you'd be sorry if you buried it, so I took it from Brown's casket. Whether it's only an expensive jewel or a harbinger of good luck, I still thought it should be passed down to Brown's descendants."

He slipped the shiny chain around the baby's neck, where the stone looked large on the child's breast. Little Bear reached a tiny hand for the necklace.

"Little Bear," Kirby said. "This is an inheritance from your father and all his Sioux forebears. Wear it proudly."

Epilogue

*L*ittle Bear walked proudly to *Wakantepee*, the highest hill on the whole Bar-C range. He could have ridden the pony Kirby had given him for his twelfth birthday, but he wanted no luxury on this special occasion. He had come to receive a vision to mark his passing from childhood into the adult world. He sought a tryst with the Great Spirit, an appointment with destiny.

He carried neither food nor water, nothing except the deerskin medicine bundle his grandfather Stuart had helped him make. His mother thought he was too young for this venture, but she had let him go after a few questions.

"My son, do you know that the Great Spirit you seek is the God of the Christians?"

He nodded.

"And to whom do you owe your salvation?"

"Jesus Christ, who died for my sins."

So his mother, knowing she had taught him well, made no further objection.

For two days Little Bear sat on the hill, patiently bearing the relentless rays of the sun. At dusk of the second day, the boy succumbed to the physical suffering of hunger and thirst and passed into oblivion, where he communed with the Great Spirit.

A brown bear walked through his vision, and appeared to him as the Great Spirit.

"What is your quest, Little Bear?" the Great One asked.

"To have courage like my father—to be a helper to my people, the Sioux."

"Do you have proof of your worthiness?"

Little Bear reached for his medicine bundle. He laid aside the bear claw his Grandmother Tatoke had given him; he paid no heed to the feather from a hawk's tail; but he held aloft a birthday gift from his mother—a long golden chain from which a black stone dangled.

"The *piedra de toque*, Great Spirit. I possess the *piedra de toque*."

"You shall have your wish, Little Bear. The Sioux are not dead; they will live again, and your quest has been granted. You will lead in the transformation of your people."

Little Bear roused from the dream world. Had it been a real vision, or just his imagination? But when he looked at the touchstone in his hand, he realized it had not been a dream. He had come here as a boy, but when he left *Wakantepee*, Little Bear was a man with a mission.

Note

T he touchstone necklace is a figment of the author's imagination and has neither factual nor mythical documentation. However, all other incidents in this book relating to Sioux culture and religion are based on facts and may be authenticated in the following references:

Allred, B. W., ed. *Great Western Indian Fights*. Lincoln, Neb.: University of Nebraska, 1960.

Brown, Dee. *Bury My Heart at Wounded Knee*. New York: Pocket Books, 1970, 1981.

The Great Chiefs. Alexandria, Va.: Time-Life Books, 1975.

Luther Standing Bear. *My People the Sioux*. Lincoln, Neb.: University of Nebraska, 1975.

Miller, David Humphreys. *Ghost Dance*. Lincoln, Neb.: University of Nebraska, 1959.

National Geographic Society. *The World of the American Indian*. Washington, D. C.: National Geographic Society, 1974.

Rosenfelt, W. E. *The Last Buffalo*. Minneapolis: T. S. Denison and Company, 1973.

Smith, Rex Alan. *Moon of Popping Trees*. Lincoln, Neb.: University of Nebraska, 1975.